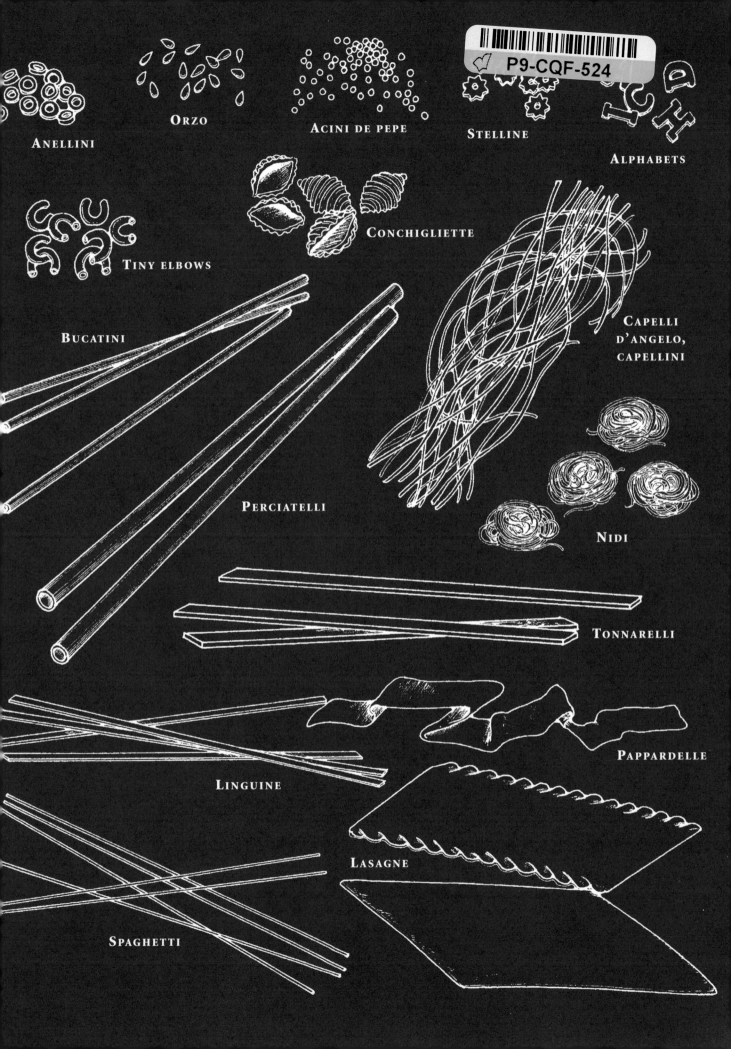

ANELLINI

ORZO

ACINI DE PEPE

STELLINE

ALPHABETS

CONCHIGLIETTE

TINY ELBOWS

BUCATINI

CAPELLI D'ANGELO, CAPELLINI

NIDI

PERCIATELLI

TONNARELLI

PAPPARDELLE

LINGUINE

LASAGNE

SPAGHETTI

VEGETARIAN

PASTA

VEGETARIAN
PASTA

An Earthly Delight Cookbook

MARLENA SPIELER

Thorsons

A Division of HarperCollinsSan Francisco

For Leah Matisse and for Bachi

Thorsons
A Division of **HarperCollins**San Francisco
HarperCollins*Publishers*

First published in paperback by Thorsons, United Kingdom, in 1993
as *200+ Vegetarian Pasta Recipes*

This edition first published 1995

HarperCollinsPublishers
1160 Battery Street, San Francisco, California 94111–1213, USA
10 East 53rd Street, New York NY 10022, USA
25 Ryde Road, Pymble, Sydney NSW 2073, Australia
31 View Road, Glenfield, Auckland 10, New Zealand
77–85 Fulham Palace Road, London W6 8JB, United Kingdom
Hazelton Lanes, 55 Avenue Road, Suite 2900, Toronto, Ontario M5R 3L2
and 1995 Markham Road, Scarborough, Ontario, M1B 5M8, Canada

No Library of Congress Cataloguing-in-Publication data available at time of printing

ISBN 0 207 18805 X

Photography by Andrew Elton
Food prepared for photography by Lynne Mullins
Styling by Karen Cotton
Kitchen assistant Emma Thomas
Illustrations by Dandi Palmer
Designed by Kerry Klinner

Printed in Hong Kong

9 8 7 6 5 4 3 2 1
99 98 97 96 95

Front cover photograph: *Chinese Noodles with Spicy Peanut Butter Sauce and Salad (p. 147)*
Back cover: *Fettuccine with Broccoli, Spinach, and Carrot Butter (p. 100)*
Page 1: *Ravioli with Sugar Snap Peas, Summer Squash, Chard, and Basil (p. 168)*
Page 2: *Pasta with Red, Yellow and Green Sweet Peppers, and Black Olives (p. 78)*
Page 3: *Rosemary-and-garlic-buttered Pasta (p. 57)*
Page 5: *Lasagne Verde, Venice-style (p. 158)*
Page 8: *Linguine alla Pizzaiola (p. 128)*
Pages 6–7: *Pasta with Green Beans, Red Sweet Peppers, Olives, Basil,
    and Pine Nuts (left) (p. 111), and Spaghettini with Provençal Onion Sauce,
    Seasoned with Capers and Tomatoes (right) (p. 106)*
Page 10: *Southeast Asian Rice Noodles with Ginger–Garlic Green Beans and Peanut Sauce (p. 147)*
Page 11: *Penne or Gnocchetti with a Pesto of Mushrooms and Black Olives (p. 124)*

Acknowledgments

For every cookbook that is written there are background eaters, dutifully tasting and chewing their way through the failures, as well as the successes. Thank you:

Leah for her gastronomical stamina when the subject was pasta for dinner.

Alan McLaughlan, for his quirky shopping trips to Berwick Street and Portobello Road, not to mention Chrisp Street.

Christine Smith, who complained only politely when for months at a time everything we ate was *al dente*.

The family Wight: Rachel and Jim, Jenny and Jo Ann, for friendship, often accompanied by pasta.

Paul Richardson for his sense of humor and friendship whichever country we meet up in; Leslie Forbes for her generosity, encouragement, and wonderful food ideas.

My family: Aunt Estelle's sophisticated taste; my mother's big platters of spaghetti; Uncle Sy's penchant for Pasta e Fagioli; my father's favorite — anything *al dente* in tomato sauce; and Bachi, for the alphabet noodle soup.

Paula Levine and Richard Hudd; Fred and Mary Barclay; Kathleen Griffen; Gretchen Spieler, who ate transcontinentally; Amanda and Tim Hamilton-Hemmeter for tales of Nigel the horse, as well as a recipe for very good tomato sauce; to Melissa and Steven Opper, who love pasta as much as I do; and Trish Robinson, Sandy Waks, and Kamala Friedman.

Freud, our garlic-smelling kitty, who sat on our laps at the dinner table and fought us for every forkful.

Thank you Sarah Sutton, always enthusiastic, always patient, editor.

Deepest thanks also to Michael Bauer, Executive Food Editor, *San Francisco Chronicle*, from whom I have learned much. I'd like to acknowledge that several of the recipes in this book have been adapted from the *San Francisco Chronicle, Bon Appetit Magazine* (USA), *Taste Magazine* (UK), and books: *From Pantry to Table* (Addison Wesley USA), *Sun-Drenched Cuisine* (Ebury UK, Tarcher USA), *Hot & Spicy* (Grafton UK, Tarcher USA), and *The Flavor of California* (Thorsons UK).

Lynne Mullins, Karen Cotton, and the publishers wish to thank the following contributors for generously supplying props for photography.

Accoutrement, Mosman, NSW
Country Road Australia
Hale Imports, Brookvale, NSW
Jim Dyer Agencies, Alexandria, NSW
G. and C. Ventura, Lilyfield, NSW

Contents

Introduction

From teething toddler to senior citizen, everyone loves pasta. The Chinese serve noodles on birthdays to signify long life; the French serve delicate pasta dishes with sauces of subtlety and grace; Eastern Europeans eat noodles sauced with peppery goulash or with sweet spices and gentle cheese; Southeast Asians with spicy, tart, and delightfully startling toppings. But it is the Italians who, rich or poor, humble or grand, eat pasta every day, with a passion. Pasta is central to the Italian drama of the dinner table, where everyday life is transcended, and the little stories and happenings of the day are related, amplified, and chewed over.

Indeed, is there any other dish that one could eat every day of the week and not grow bored with? Pasta is consummately versatile and can be served with whatever the garden or market has to offer. The most delicious of pasta dishes are often the simple ones, born of necessity, and made from the frugal ingredients a cook might have on hand. Then there is the other delicious extreme: pasta splashed with rich cream or rare ingredients, such as wild mushrooms or truffles.

And the pasta itself comes in an endless variety of sizes and shapes, from supple strands to flat, wide noodles; from chunky, chewy tubes to curly worm-like shapes; tiny nuggets the size and shape of rice or letters of the alphabet, to even smaller ones the size of peppercorns, and so on, *ad infinitum*. I've seen heart-shaped pasta for Valentine's Day, stars for national holidays, Christmas trees, and funny faces or little people shapes for children to amuse themselves with.

While pasta is usually prepared from wheat flour, it may also be made from a wide variety of other grains and flavored with a near endless selection of vegetables, herbs, and so on. Whole-wheat (wholemeal), buckwheat, rice, mung beans, yam flour, ground corn, vegetable powders such as artichoke, tomato, beet (beetroot) — the list goes on and on. Natural foods shops often have a good selection, as do ethnic markets. Recently, in London's Chinatown, I made a delightful discovery of flat, dried rice noodles tinted to various pastel hues with vegetable mixtures.

Pasta can be prepared in a wide variety of ways, too: floating in broth, tossed with savory vegetables, cloaked in silken cream, stir-fried into chow mein.

High carbohydrate, low-fat, and inexpensive, pasta is as healthfully sustaining and as economical as the ingredients with which it shares the pot.

A Short History of Pasta

Though some claim that Marco Polo brought pasta from China to Italy, and hence Europe, we know that this is not true. Marco Polo returned from his Asian travels in 1292 and records of pasta-eating in Italy date from much earlier than that. Indeed, it is likely that pasta actually originated in the Middle East and spread to other areas from there. The first pasta was a pounded paste of toasted grains eaten in Neolithic times; eventually this paste was boiled into dumpling shapes, much like modern pasta.

From the Middle East it spread east and west, north and south. One of the first records of pasta-eating in Italy is a 4th-century bas-relief from a tomb outside Rome, showing pasta-making tools which look remarkably like the ones used today.

By the 15th century a huge variety of pasta existed in Italy, and the popularity of noodles and dumplings was spreading throughout Europe.

In the 18th century Thomas Jefferson brought pasta to the New World after having fallen in love with it in Italy. He took a pasta machine and some Parmesan cheese back to Washington so that his cook could prepare his favorite food.

Waves of Italian immigrants, as well as those from Germany and Sweden, brought their pasta dishes to America's culinary melting pot and today pasta is one of the national dishes of the United States.

Pasta is universally loved in Australia and Britain, where the one-time national dish of 'spag bol' has given way to a wide range of pastas, tossed together with fresh vegetables, savory oils and seasonings.

Pasta can be a humble dish for everyday nurturing, or an elegant dish of great sophistication. In this collection of recipes I have tried to include a little of everything, from rich to lean, simple to complex, traditional to innovative. The array of luscious meals one can prepare with pasta is virtually endless.

Notes on the Recipes

Measurements are given in American, imperial, and metric. While American measurements are usually given in volume measures (i.e. cups) rather than weights, I have indicated amounts of uncooked pasta by weight because that is how it is sold. Since most dried pasta is sold in 1-lb (500-g) packages, 4 oz. (125 g) of pasta roughly indicates a quarter of the package; if the package is of a different weight, adjust accordingly.

In the conversions I have also taken a few liberties on behalf of ease of preparation. For the soups, I call for 4 cups of broth or water in U.S. measurements, 1¾ imperial pints or 1 litre in the British and Australian. While the amounts are not exactly equal, they are close enough that there should be no problems. If any soup seems too dry or too watery, adjust the liquid to suit your own taste.

All garlic means large cloves, as I believe one can never have too much garlic. I do admit, however, that the amounts of garlic in many of my recipes could be too much for some readers' taste — for those who don't share my passion, reduce the amount to suit your own palate.

All olive oil is extra virgin or as full-flavored an oil as you can find.

Vegetable broth, in a perfect world, means homemade and very flavorful broth (see p. 15). In my less-than-perfect world, vegetable broth often means hot water mixed with a bouillon (stock) cube or two, unless otherwise noted.

Do not use ready-grated Parmesan cheese, use a chunk of fresh Parmesan cheese and grate it yourself, or have it grated for you. If you cannot get a whole chunk of Parmesan, it is better to use a humbler cheese than a pre-grated Parmesan. A number of cheeses are delicious for grating and much less expensive than Parmesan: Romano, locatelli, pecorino, Asiago, and dried Jack. There are also various less expensive Parmesans, such as a very nice one from South America and another from Australia.

Serving portions are indicated in the recipes but are highly subjective. When it comes to pasta, what constitutes a meal-sized portion for one person might be no more than a snack for someone else. It also depends on what else is on your menu, and whether the pasta is to be a first course, a soup, or a main dish. When in doubt, use your own judgment about your own and your fellow eaters' appetites.

A World Guide to Pasta

ITALIAN PASTA

Italian pasta — a simple mixture of flour and water — is pounded, rolled, and extruded into an assortment of shapes with melodic-sounding names and usually whimsical and playful meanings, such as radiatori (little radiators), vermicelli (little worms), and farfalle (butterflies) to name a few.

The differing shapes all lend themselves in different ways to the wide variety of sauces and toppings: thin strands of pasta, such as spaghetti or vermicelli, taste best with lively, vivacious sauces, while flat pasta is good with almost everything, especially richer sauces that can settle on it, and pastina (tiny pasta shapes) are best in soup or pilaf-type mixtures. Thick pasta tastes best with robust, feisty sauces, while thinner, more delicate pasta is good with light, subtle sauces. And stuffed pasta is best sauced simply, as its filling is like an inside-out sauce, giving flavor and texture from the inside, rather than as a topping. Such a diversity of shapes gives great variety to what is basically a very simple food.

FRESH PASTA

Fresh pasta at its best is tender and silky, yet also supple and yielding to the teeth. It is quite different from *pasta asciutta* (dried pasta) which should be cooked *al dente,* that is, so that it is somewhat resistant to the teeth. That hearty, chewy quality is a result of using semolina flour, and extruding the pasta through a specially created machine. But when you make pasta at home you want to produce a smooth, tender noodle, the sort that is expensive or difficult to come by in the shops. This can be achieved by using plain flour and lots of eggs and rolling the dough rather than extruding it (although a number of pasta machines for domestic use are based on extruding). Rolling the dough may be done either by hand with a heavy roller — hard, hard work — or run through the classic hand-rolling pasta machine. I recommend the latter. When making your own pasta you can use a number of vegetable or herb colorings and flavorings: pesto, saffron, hot peppers, and so on.

Fresh Pasta

2 cups (1 lb, 500 g) plain flour, preferably
    unbleached
3 eggs
½ teaspoon salt

Place the flour in a mound on a large floured board or in a large bowl. Make a hollow in the centre large enough to hold the eggs (I do this by placing my fist in the top of the mound and moving it until it forms a generous well).

Crack open the eggs into the well, add the salt, and beat the eggs with a fork, incorporating a small amount of flour as you go along. Use your free hand to keep the walls of flour upright and to keep the eggs from dribbling out. Gradually, all the flour will be incorporated. Towards the end you can just use your hands to mix it.

Knead the dough by hand for about 5–10 minutes, or in a food processor for about 20 seconds. It should be elastic and smooth and should not break apart sharply when pulled. Place in a bowl or plastic bag that has been lightly oiled with olive oil, cover or seal, and leave for at least 30 minutes to tenderize the dough. You can store this in the refrigerator for up to two days.

Roll the pasta by breaking off a walnut-sized piece of dough, flattening it enough to fit in the large size of the roller on your pasta machine. Roll it through once, then fold it and roll it through again. Gradually reduced the size of the roller until you achieve the desired thinness.

Use the pasta in whole sheets, or cut it to the width desired, either using the cutters on the machine or by hand; toss with flour then place on a board. Alternatively you may dry the pasta over a chair or pole. It does not need to dry for long; it should retain its moist freshness.

To cook, boil the pasta in rapidly boiling salted water until tender (about 2–3 minutes).

VARIATIONS

White Wine Pasta: In place of one of the eggs, add 2–3 tablespoons of dry white wine and 1 tablespoon of olive oil. This makes a silky, suave pasta.

Pesto Pasta: In place of one of the eggs, use 1 tablespoon pesto (see p. 16); alternatively, use 3 eggs and incorporate powdered pesto (available in America) into the flour.

Ginger Pasta: Add 3 tablespoons of freshly grated ginger root along with the eggs.

Hot Red Chili Pepper Pasta: Mix 3 tablespoons of cayenne pepper or hot red chili pepper powder into the flour.

Saffron: Add ½ teaspoon of saffron to the eggs.

Corn Pasta: Substitute ½ cup (4 oz., 125 g) of cornmeal for an equal amount of flour, and add ½ cup (4 oz., 125 g) of puréed sweet corn with the eggs.

Rosemary Pasta: Add several tablespoons of chopped fresh rosemary with the eggs.

Chive Pasta: Add chopped chives with the eggs.

DRIED PASTA

Dried Pasta, or *pasta asciutta*, made from semolina and water, is chewy and supple and utterly satisfying. It should swell up as it absorbs the hot water in which it is cooked and should remain firm to the teeth, or *al dente;* it should never sink and become flabby.

How to Cook Dried Pasta

Dried pasta may be cooked either by boiling for the whole cooking time or by boiling for a short while, then steeping it in the hot water. The most important thing to remember is never to overcook it. Because the pasta continues to cook in its own heat while you transfer it to the colander to drain, remove it from the stove just before it reaches the state you desire.

Do not rinse drained pasta with cold water, unless the pasta is to be used later, for example in a salad. Instead, toss the drained pasta back into the pot with a drizzle of olive oil. I often add a clove of chopped garlic, too, and find that pasta seasoned with garlic and olive oil adds another dimension to any sauce that goes over it, especially a tomato and vegetable one.

An old wives' tale claims that the way to test pasta is to fling a few strands at the wall — if it sticks, the pasta is done. This was recently debunked by aficionados who said that if the pasta stuck to the wall it was overcooked. But it actually does work pretty well; just make sure that once you check the pasta by flinging it, the rest doesn't get a chance to overcook as it sits in the pot. To fling or not to fling is up to you; for accuracy, however, I recommend tasting a piece or two of pasta as you go along, and judging the 'doneness' with your teeth. But for fun, I recommend throwing that pasta at the wall.

METHOD ONE:

Add the pasta to a large pot of rapidly boiling salted water (add the salt after the water has come to the boil for a fresher taste) and boil until *al dente*. I don't recommend adding oil to the water as it tends to just sit on top of the water during cooking and has no effect on the pasta beneath. The cooking time will depend upon the size and type of pasta. Use the package directions as a guide, but I find that the recommended times are usually too long, resulting in overcooked pasta. You must check the pasta every so often to be sure, then drain it just when the pasta approaches firm-to-the-tooth but is no longer hard and crunchy inside.

METHOD TWO:

This method results in a particularly toothsome, plump but firm pasta and is suited to sturdier shapes, such as spaghetti or penne, rather than thin, delicate ones or fresh pasta. First, add the pasta to a large pot filled with rapidly boiling salted water and boil for 2 minutes. Turn off the heat, cover, and leave to steep. Spaghetti takes about 6–8 minutes of steeping, other shapes vary. You will have to taste the pasta occasionally to ascertain the exact moment it is ready. Pasta can overcook by the steeping method as easily as it can by boiling.

FAR EASTERN PASTA

Cellophane noodles: these Chinese transparent noodles may be made from either mung beans (when they are called bean threads) or potato starch. Japanese transparent noodles are called *shirataki* and are made of yam flour.

Both need to be soaked before cooking: soak the Chinese noodles for about 10 minutes in hot but not boiling water, then boil for about 3 minutes. The Japanese noodles will need about 20 to 25 minutes' soaking before being boiled for 3 minutes. Look for these in Chinese and other Far Eastern stores.

Chinese egg noodles (mein): most supermarkets stock several types of dried Chinese noodles. They cook in a very short time, depending on their thickness, so check for 'doneness' after about 3 minutes.

Chinese grocers usually stock fresh mein, and often in a wide variety of thicknesses. Fresh ones cook even quicker — 1 minute will do for the thinner ones.

Udon: these thick, fresh Japanese noodles are usually available in vacuum packs from shops specialising in Japanese ingredients. They are often packed in one-portion, snack-sized parcels. Udon may be whole-wheat (wholemeal) or white, with cooking times and directions given on the package.

Soba: are thin, dried Japanese buckwheat noodles that cook very quickly. They may be thread thin or flat and almost fettuccine-like in shape. (I prefer the latter.)

Somen: these are thin Japanese noodles that cook very quickly and are most suitable for soups.

Ramen: the dried noodles in a packet with powdered broth are ramen. They come with a wide variety of fillings and make a savory snack or light meal when garnished with a handful of something fresh: a few bean sprouts, fresh coriander leaves, or scallions (spring onions). Browned in a little butter or oil they make a delicious basis for a salad (see Aunt Estelle's Napa Cabbage Salad with Crunchy Noodles and Nuts, p. 43).

Rice sticks: thin, dried rice noodles, also called rice vermicelli or *py mei fun*. They are wiry and twig-like, and may be either boiled until fluffy and soft, or deep-fried into crisp, puffy, serpent shapes.

To boil, soak in cold water for 10 minutes, or follow the directions on the packet.

To fry to a crispy cloudlike shape, deep-fry at about 375°F (190°C) until they puff up. Remove from the hot oil immediately after they have puffed up, before they even hint at browning or turning golden, as that detracts from their delicate taste and light, crisp texture.

Rice noodles: available dried and fresh from Chinese grocers. When fresh they are called *chow fun*. They are bland and soft, tasting of rice, and pleasingly tender to the teeth. Since they are quite delicate, they should be cooked — usually stir-fried — on the day of purchase, or at least within two days.

To make chow fun with vegetables, first stir-fry them in a very hot wok, then remove and set aside. Stir-fry the vegetables, then combine the two mixtures along with a small amount of seasoning sauce. (See Broccoli Chow Fun on p. 146.)

Dried rice noodles are flat and thin and are often imported from Vietnam or Thailand. These are sometimes also called rice vermicelli or rice sticks, but they are much wider than vermicelli. Soak in cold water for about 15 minutes, then boil until just tender (only a few minutes).

BASIC RECIPES

Leftover Pasta

Leftover pasta is different from freshly cooked pasta. Many Italians claim it is good only to feed to the animals. (In Italy you will often see a little pile of leftover pasta on a piece of newspaper on the ground, a crowd of mewing felines pawing at the strands of spaghetti, chewing at whatever they are lucky enough to get a mouthful of.)

However, others, myself included, find leftover pasta quite tempting, especially as a solitary snack or late night supper. Some dishes are fine just reheated in a few spoonfuls of water, tossed quickly over medium to high heat, and forked up as a midnight feast. But for more social eating experiences, omelettes or frittatas are an excellent way of using up leftover pasta.

Pasta Frittata

I vary this frittata every time I make it, usually by adding toppings of basil pesto or red sun-dried tomato pesto, or spicy Mexican-style salsas.

2 garlic cloves, chopped
about 1 tablespoon olive oil
2 portions leftover sauced pasta with vegetables
4 eggs, lightly beaten
salt and freshly ground black pepper, to taste
4 oz. (125 g) cheese such as Cheddar, mozzarella, fontina, etc., or a combination that includes Parmesan, grated
several large pinches of dried herbs, such as oregano or mixed herbs or chopped fresh herbs, such as basil or rosemary

Gently warm the garlic in the olive oil in a large skillet (frying pan).

Meanwhile, combine the pasta and vegetables with the eggs. Season with salt and pepper. Pour into the pan, then cook over low to medium heat until the underneath is a golden color and the top is more or less set.

Arrange the cheese on top and broil (grill) until melted. Serve immediately, sprinkled with herbs of choice.

SERVES 2–4

Pasta e Fagioli
(Hearty Soup–Stew with Beans)

Leftover tomato-and-vegetable-sauced pasta tossed into a pot with some garlic-flavored oil, a little vegetable broth and some beans makes a hearty soup–stew, perfect for supper or midnight feasting.

3 garlic cloves, coarsely chopped
1 small carrot, finely diced
2–3 tablespoons olive oil
any leftover plain blanched vegetables, if available: zucchini (courgettes), chard (silver beet), etc.
3 portions leftover sauced pasta, with vegetables such as peas, etc.
8 oz. (250 g) cooked or drained tinned beans, such as red kidney, borlotti, white kidney (cannellini), or chickpeas
2 cups (16 fl. oz., 500 ml) vegetable broth, or as needed (see p. 15)
salt and freshly ground black pepper, to taste
generous handful of fresh herbs or pinches of dried herbs (fresh rosemary, crumbled mixed herbs, basil), pesto, whatever is available
freshly grated Parmesan cheese, to serve

Lightly cook the garlic and carrot in the olive oil until the garlic is golden and the carrot softened, then add the vegetables and pasta. Toss it all in the oil, then add the beans and let it all cook for a few minutes to absorb the garlic-scented oil.

Add the broth, then cook uncovered over medium to high heat until soupy, adding more broth if needed. Do not stir; merely turn once or twice. Season with salt and pepper.

Serve hot, sprinkled with herbs of choice or with spoonfuls of pesto, and with grated cheese.

SERVES ABOUT 4, DEPENDING ON THE LEFTOVERS

RIGHT ♦ *Pasta e Fagioli (Hearty Soup–Stew with Beans)*

Vegetable Broth 1

The most frugal of vegetable broths are also the most delicious, consisting of vegetable trimmings and/or leftover vegetable cooking liquid with a handful of aromatics. A bouillon (stock) cube or two in lieu of salt makes the broth rich and flavorful. The water left from cooking fresh-tasting vegetables makes the best broth. Do not use the water from cabbage or other strong-smelling vegetables. Adding whole cloves of garlic makes a gently fragrant broth, as garlic loses its strong scent as it simmers.

4 cups (1¾ imp. pints, 1 litre) liquid (from cooking vegetables, plus enough water to make up 4 cups)
vegetable trimmings: celery, carrot, leeks, turnips, tomatoes, parsley, zucchini (courgettes), red sweet peppers (capsicums), potato peelings
6 whole garlic cloves, unpeeled (or less, to taste) or 1 small onion, cut into quarters
a few sprigs of parsley or other fresh herbs
2–3 bouillon (stock) cubes

Combine all the ingredients. Bring to the boil, then reduce the heat and simmer for 15–20 minutes, or until the garlic is tender.

Strain and use as desired.

Vegetable Broth 2

4 cups (1¾ imp. pints, 1 litre) water
1 onion, quartered
2 celery stalks, cut into bite-sized pieces
2 carrots, cut into bite-sized pieces
handful of parsley, dill, or other herb
2–3 bouillon (stock) cubes

Combine all the ingredients. Bring to the boil, then reduce the heat and simmer for 20 minutes, or until the carrots and celery are tender.

Strain or keep the vegetables in the broth, as you wish.

Pesto alla Genovese

This garlicky, herby balm from Genoa is delicious spooned into soups, spread on crusty bread for sandwiches and, of course, as a topping for a wide variety of pasta dishes.

4–6 garlic cloves, finely chopped
1½ oz. (45 g) pine nuts
8 oz. (250 g) basil leaves
½ cup (4 fl. oz., 125 ml) olive oil
2 oz. (60 g) Parmesan, Pecorino, or other similar
   cheese, freshly grated
pinch of salt

Process the garlic in a blender (liquidizer) or food processor, or pound in a mortar and pestle. Add the pine nuts, crush, then add the basil leaves and either process or pound. Slowly add the olive oil, working the mixture into a thick and pungent paste. Add cheese and salt to taste.

Use immediately or refrigerate for up to 2 weeks. It can also be frozen.

MAKES ABOUT 1½ CUPS
(12 FL. OZ., 375 ML)

Red Pesto

A zesty, relish-like sauce, halfway between classic pesto and an Italian salsa. This recipe comes from my book The Flavor of California *(Thorsons, 1994). Enjoy red pesto either on its own or with other sauces.*

4 garlic cloves, finely chopped
15 oil-marinated sun-dried tomatoes, diced
6–8 ripe fresh or tinned tomatoes, chopped
3 fl. oz. (90 ml) oil from the jar of sun-dried
   tomatoes (make up with olive oil if necessary)
½–1 oz. (15–30 g) fresh basil, coarsely chopped

Combine all ingredients in a blender (liquidizer) or food processor or by hand, and mix well until your mixture is like a chunky sauce.

Use immediately or keep refrigerated for up to 3 days.

MAKES ABOUT 1½ CUPS
(12 FL. OZ., 375 ML)

ABOVE ♦ *Olio Santo (top), Pesto alla Genovese (left), and Quick Garlicky Tomato Sauce (right)*

Olio Santo (Olive Oil Seasoned with Hot Chili Peppers and Herbs)

Olio Santo is the Tuscan preparation of dried hot peppers and basil steeped in olive oil. Traditionally used as a last-minute seasoning drizzled onto pasta and robust soups, I find it is also good on salads and pizza.

2 cups (16 fl. oz., 500 ml) olive oil
5 small, dried, hot red chili peppers
about 20 fresh basil leaves

Pour the olive oil into a clean jar or bottle. Add the chili peppers and basil and leave in a dark place. The flavor develops with time, but is also good after only a few days.

VARIATIONS
Chilied Olive Oil: Omit the herbs.
Minted Olive Oil: Substitute about 10 fresh mint leaves and 1–2 teaspoons of dried mixed herbs for the basil.
Garlic Olive Oil: Chopped or sliced garlic steeped in olive oil makes a delicious Tuscan flavoring for pasta, roasted sweet peppers, salads, pizza, and so on. Do not leave the garlic in the oil for longer than 2 weeks, though, as it can breed dangerous toxins. It is so delicious, however, that it will probably not last long enough for this to be a consideration.

MAKES ABOUT 2 CUPS
(16 FL. OZ., 500 ML)

Quick Garlicky Tomato Sauce

4 garlic cloves, chopped
2 tablespoons olive oil
2 cups (16 fl. oz., 500 ml) tomato purée (passata)
large pinch of fennel seeds
large pinch of dried mixed herbs
salt and freshly ground black pepper, to taste
pinch of sugar (optional)

Lightly sauté the garlic in the olive oil until the garlic becomes fragrant, then pour in the tomato purée.

Simmer for 5–10 minutes; season with the fennel seeds and dried herbs, salt and pepper, and sugar (if using).

Béchamel Sauce

1 oz. (30 g) butter
2 tablespoons flour
2 cups (16 fl. oz., 500 ml) hot (not boiling) milk
salt and freshly ground black pepper, to taste
freshly grated nutmeg, to taste

Melt the butter in a pan and sprinkle in the flour. Cook for a few moments, until the flour is golden, then remove from the heat and gradually stir in the milk, a little at a time.

Return to a medium heat and bring to the boil, then cook, stirring, until the sauce thickens. Season with salt, pepper, and nutmeg.

Dried Mushrooms

Dried mushrooms provide a delicious, strong, and versatile flavor addition in the pasta kitchen. There are a wide variety of mushrooms (and other fungi) available, but the most easily found are the shiitake (Chinese black mushroom), the Italian porcini, the French cèpe, or the almost smoky-flavored morel.

Dried mushrooms are often more flavorful than their fresh counterparts as their flavors and aromas have been intensified by the drying process; when rehydrated they still seem to have more flavor than the originals, and you have the added bonus of the soaking liquid, which gives delicious flavor to any recipe.

Other fungi, such as the Chinese tree cloud fungus or wood ears, may be rehydrated by the same method as below, but their soaking liquid is not as flavorful as that of the mushrooms.

Place the dried mushrooms in a bowl and pour hot (but not boiling) broth or water over. Cover and leave for about 30 minutes.

When cool enough to handle, squeeze the mushrooms over the soaking bowl, then strain all the liquid, discarding the sandy debris. The liquid can be kept (it freezes well) and used for soups or sauces if it is not needed in the recipe.

Soak the mushrooms for a few minutes in cold water, swishing them around a bit to dislodge any grit still clinging to them, then squeeze again. Discard this liquid, which is not as flavorful as the liquid from the first soaking. Proceed as directed in the recipe.

Sun-dried Tomatoes

In parts of Italy's south you will see the sweet fruit halved and set in the midday sun to dry on wire beds. Sun-dried tomatoes are originally Italian, but are now to be found in much contemporary Mediterranean-inspired fare. Once dry they are chewy and slightly cardboard-like; if you nibble one in this state you will wonder what all the fuss is about. To bring out their special flavor they must be rehydrated and either marinated with garlic and olive oil, or cooked, to add a savory accent to other ingredients.

Alternatively, sun-dried tomatoes may be purchased marinated in olive oil. They are delicious, and have the added bonus of their seasoned oil, which makes a great addition to pasta, sauces, or salads. Store-bought marinated sun-dried tomatoes will last quite well in the refrigerator, but home-made ones will not — I'm not sure why, but I suspect that the salt content of the commercially produced ones has something to do with it.

To rehydrate dried tomatoes, place them in a saucepan with water to cover and bring to the boil. Reduce the heat and simmer for 15 minutes, or until the tomatoes plump up. Drain (reserve the water for another use, if you like), and add the tomatoes to pasta sauces, stews, soups, etc.

To marinate the rehydrated and drained tomatoes, place them in a bowl with chopped garlic and fresh basil or thyme to taste, a generous sprinkling of salt (unless they have already been salted before drying), a splash of balsamic or red wine vinegar and olive oil to cover. Let the mixture stand for at least an hour, then serve as an antipasto or a snack with bread. The mixture will keep for several days in the refrigerator.

Preparing Fresh Artichokes

Artichokes are often served whole, boiled or steamed; the leaves are pulled off one by one, dipped into melted butter or a mayonnaise-type sauce, then scraped with the teeth to eat the tiny bit of delicate artichoke flesh at the base. The inner heart is then exposed (its choke removed) and the essence of the artichoke is yours to enjoy. But for soups, stews, sauces, and pasta recipes that use fresh artichokes, you must rid each of its sharp leaves and pare it down to its tender heart.
While tinned and frozen artichoke hearts are readily available, it is worth knowing how to prepare fresh ones: their subtle, rich, and distinctive flavor is incomparable.

Cut off the stem of each artichoke and peel to remove the stringy fibers. Often the stems are delicious, sometimes they are not. Cook them anyway and decide later whether you want to use them.

Trim the bottom of the artichoke, paring away the tough outer covering, then begin removing the leaves by pulling each back until it snaps off. The edible portion, or most of it, will remain. Discard the leaves.

When you reach the more tender inner leaves, cut off their sharp tops but leave the edible bottom part. Trim the edges where you have pulled the leaves off. You now have an artichoke heart. Some artichoke hearts do not have much of an inner fuzzy choke and may be eaten whole, but others have large inedible chokes which need to be removed. To do this, cut each heart in half or quarters and, with a sharp paring knife, cut out the choke.

Place the artichoke heart in a saucepan of acidulated water (water to which either the juice of half a lemon or a spoonful of flour has been added). This will prevent the artichokes discoloring. Bring to the boil and cook until just tender. Cooking time will depend upon the size and age of the artichokes, but halves or quarters should take 10–15 minutes. Drain and use as directed by the recipe.

Roasted Tomatoes

Roasting intensifies the flavor of tomatoes and caramelizes the juices. They make an almost instant sauce for pasta, combined with other simple seasonings such as olive oil, garlic, capers, hot chili pepper, etc., or a delicious basis for sauces and soups. Tomatoes may be roasted in advance and kept in the refrigerator, well covered, for up to 5 days.

Place a single layer of small to medium tomatoes in the bottom of a heavy casserole or baking dish, leaving enough room to turn the tomatoes. Place under the broiler (grill) and broil until the tops of the tomatoes char a bit and their skins begin to split. Remove from the broiler and gently turn the tomatoes charred side down.

Bake in the oven at 400°F (200°C) for approximately 40 minutes, until the tomatoes are charred all over and some of the juices have trickled out and caramelized.

Remove from the oven and leave to cool (the juices will be thin at first and thicken as they cool). Before using, remove the skins, which will just slip off, and dice the tomato flesh, then combine with the thickened juices .

Roasted Sweet Peppers

Roasting or broiling (grilling) transforms the crunchy fresh sweet pepper (capsicum) into a completely different vegetable: tender and almost silky in texture, with a smoky nuance. Red, yellow, and green sweet peppers all roast to distinctly different flavors: red and yellow become sweet, green peppers strong-flavored and very vegetal.

Roasted sweet peppers make the basis of wonderful salads, soups, sandwich fillings, sauces and the like, and seem to be at their best when combined with pasta.

Roast the sweet peppers over an open flame on top of the stove (cooker) or under a hot broiler (grill) for about 6 minutes on each side, until they are charred in spots and the flesh has softened.

Place in a paper or plastic bag and seal, or place in a bowl and cover. This creates steam, which helps loosen the skin. Leave for about 20 minutes.

Peel away and discard the skin. Clean and deseed the peppers, then proceed as directed in the recipe.

Above ♦ *Roasted Sweet Peppers*

Soups and Stews

Pasta is traditionally served
in soups the world over, whether floating in broths of sparkling clarity
or simmered in savory vegetable-filled potages. Often a handful of pasta is added
to the soup at the last minute to cook in the broth and absorb its flavors,
or the soup might be served ladled over
cooked pasta.

◆ ◆ ◆

*Stuffed pasta is traditionally served
in broth in various cultures, either Italian style, with freshly grated
Parmesan cheese, or Chinese style, with wonton as the pasta of choice and a final fillip
of sesame oil and soy sauce. But plain pasta is delicious in broth too,
or added to nearly any light soup
to give it body.*

♦ ♦ ♦

Roasted Tomato and Garlic Broth with Green Beans and Stelline (Tiny Stars)

*Clear and savory, this is a lovely soup: flavorful enough to
satisfy, yet light enough not to weigh you down.
The simple broth is created by sautéing garlic then adding
diced, roasted tomatoes and broth. That is all there is to it,
but it packs a deliciously strong flavor wallop. Tiny pasta
such as stelline seems to taste best, and it looks delightful too,
but if unavailable use thin pasta strands such as capellini,
or even broken spaghettini.*

9 medium or 12 small tomatoes
3 garlic cloves, coarsely chopped
1–2 tablespoons extra virgin olive oil
handful of green beans, cut into bite-sized lengths
4 cups (1¾ imp. pints, 1 litre) vegetable broth
   (see p. 15)
6 oz. (185 g) stelline or other tiny pasta

Roast the tomatoes as described on page 18.

Sauté the garlic in the olive oil until lightly gilded; add
the green beans and cook for 1–2 minutes, then add the
tomatoes and their cooking juice. Pour in the vegetable
broth and bring to the boil.

Meanwhile, cook the pasta until just tender; drain.

Serve each bowl of soup with several spoonfuls of
cooked pasta stirred in.

VARIATION

Chilied Roasted Tomato and Green Bean Broth:
This Mexican variation has a spicy kick but is not
uncomfortably hot. Add a teaspoon or so of mild chili
pepper powder to taste, when the soup is finished. Serve
ladled over thin strands of cooked capellini instead of the
star-shaped stelline.

SERVES 4

Goan Ginger-scented Tomato and Cabbage Soup with Small Pasta and Fresh Mint

*This fragrant soup is satisfying but not heavy and hails from
Goa, where Indian spicing, such as ginger, is often combined
with Portuguese seasoning, such as fresh mint. It makes an
excellent first course.*

4 oz. (125 g) small pasta, such as alphabets,
   or short, thick-cut pasta
2 onions, coarsely chopped
3–5 garlic cloves, coarsely chopped
1 oz. (30 g) butter
2 teaspoons ground ginger
1 small carrot, diced
14 oz. (435 g) diced fresh or tinned tomatoes
6 cups (2½ imp. pints, 1.5 litres) vegetable broth
   (see p. 15)
½ white cabbage, very thinly sliced
10–15 fresh mint leaves, very thinly sliced
salt and freshly ground black pepper, or cayenne
   pepper, to taste

Cook the pasta until *al dente;* drain and set aside.

Lightly sauté the onion and garlic in the butter until
softened. Stir in the ginger and carrot and cook for a few
moments; add the tomatoes, vegetable broth, and
cabbage. Cook over medium heat until the vegetables are
tender (about 15–20 minutes). Adjust the seasoning with
salt and black or cayenne pepper, adding more ginger if
needed.

Ladle the soup over several spoonfuls of pasta per
person. Season each portion with a sprinkling of fresh
mint and serve immediately.

SERVES 4

*PREVIOUS PAGE ♦ Green Vegetable Soup with Pesto (left),
Broccoli and Pastina in Garlic Broth (centre), and Goan
Ginger-scented Tomato and Cabbage Soup with Small Pasta
and Fresh Mint
RIGHT ♦ Roasted Tomato and Garlic Broth with Green Beans
and Stelline (Tiny Stars)*

Green Vegetable Soup with Pesto

Short, thick pasta bubbles in the pot along with a selection of green vegetables, the broth enriched by the last-minute addition of that intensely flavored basil and garlic paste — pesto. Don't be tempted to add everything from the garden to the soup; it is at its best when only green vegetables are used. Take care also not to cook or overheat the pesto once it has been added to the soup — cooking it dilutes and dulls its fresh, sassy flavor.

4 oz. (125 g) ditalini or other short, fat pasta
2 garlic cloves, coarsely chopped
2 tablespoons extra virgin olive oil
2 tablespoons flour
4 cups (1¾ imp. pints, 1 litre) vegetable broth
　(see p. 15)
4–5 cabbage leaves, blanched and thinly sliced
　(optional)
4–5 oz. (125–155 g) cooked chopped fresh,
　or frozen, spinach (weight after cooking)
3–4 oz. (90–125 g) fresh and blanched, or frozen,
　peas
4 heaped tablespoons pesto (see p. 16), or to taste

Cook the pasta in rapidly boiling salted water until *al dente*. Drain and set aside.

Lightly sauté the garlic in the olive oil until just gilded, then sprinkle in the flour and cook out its rawness for just a few moments.

Off the heat, stir in the stock, then return to the heat and cook for several minutes until slightly thickened. Add the cabbage leaves (if using), spinach, and peas and cook through.

Just before serving, add the cooked paste and heat through. Serve with a spoonful of fragrant pesto stirred into each bowl.

SERVES 4

Spicy Pumpkin Soup with Thin Pasta

This French soup has an overlay of Latin American flavors.

4 garlic cloves, chopped
5 scallions (spring onions) or shallots, chopped
1 oz. (30 g) butter
1 tablespoon flour
1 red sweet pepper (capsicum), diced
1 lb (500 g) pumpkin, peeled and diced
1 tablespoon mild chili pepper powder
2 teaspoons paprika
½ teaspoon cumin
¼ teaspoon dried oregano leaves, crushed
8 fl. oz. (250 ml) tomato purée (passata), or
　8 diced fresh tomatoes, or 14-oz. (435-g) tin
　chopped tomatoes
3 cups (24 fl. oz., 750 ml) vegetable broth
　(see p. 15)
4 oz. (125 g) thin pasta, such as spaghettini, etc.
8 fl. oz. (250 ml) milk
14 oz. (435 g) cooked or tinned cannellini (white
　kidney) beans, drained
salt and cayenne pepper, to taste
freshly grated Parmesan or other hard cheese to serve
thinly sliced scallions (spring onions) or fresh
　coriander leaves to serve (optional)

Lightly sauté the garlic and scallions or shallots in the butter; sprinkle in the flour and cook for a few minutes. Add the red sweet pepper and pumpkin and cook for a few minutes. Add the chili pepper powder, paprika, cumin, and oregano and cook for just a few moments.

Add the tomato purée, sauce or tomatoes, and broth; bring to the boil, then cover and simmer until the pumpkin is tender. Purée half the mixture and return it to the pan, so that you have an uneven texture.

Add the pasta and cook until *al dente*. If using very thin pasta, cook it directly in the soup; if using thicker pasta, such as spaghetti, first cook it in boiling water until half-done, then drain and add to the soup.

When the pasta is nearly tender add the milk and beans to the soup and heat through. Season with salt and cayenne pepper and serve hot, sprinkled with cheese, and with thinly sliced scallions or coriander, if desired.

SERVES 4–6

Creamy Onion Soup with Tiny Pasta

This rich soup begins like French onion soup: browned onions and broth, simmered for a long time until dark and sweetly fragrant. But you add just enough cream to take the edge off the onions, and instead of serving the soup over a cheese-topped croûte, you serve it ladled over al dente orzo or other small pasta, and blanketed with grated cheese.

10 onions, coarsely chopped

1 oz. (30 g) butter

4 cups (1¾ imp. pints, 1 litre) vegetable broth
   (see p. 15)

4 fl. oz. (125 ml) light (single) cream

1 egg, lightly beaten

8 oz. (250 g) orzo or other small pasta, or thin
   pasta such as capellini, broken into short lengths

3 oz. (90 g) Parmesan cheese, freshly grated

Lightly sauté the onions in the butter long and slowly, until they caramelize and turn first golden, then light brown. It will take about 30 minutes, at least, probably longer.

Add the broth and bring to the boil; reduce the heat and simmer for at least an hour, preferably longer, or until the broth is richly flavored.

Combine the cream and egg, then lighten the mixture by adding a ladleful or two of the broth. Stir this back into the onion soup and simmer for a few minutes over low to medium heat, but do not allow it to come to the boil.

Meanwhile, cook the pasta until *al dente*; drain.

Serve the soup poured over the pasta, each portion sprinkled with a generous amount of Parmesan cheese.

SERVES 4–6

BELOW ♦ *Spicy Pumpkin Soup with Thin Pasta*

Mediterranean Roasted Vegetable Soup–Stew

I devised this robust, full-of-Mediterranean-flavor soup–stew during a winter holiday in the mountains of Ibiza. With the weather cold and grim, our main activity was going not to the beach, as we had envisioned, but to the market, and cooking and eating ourselves into delicious oblivion.
This soup resulted from a casserole full of leftover vegetables; in fact this is an ideal way of using up such leftovers. Our vegetables had been grilled over an open fire, and the smoky nuances gave it added depth, but if outdoor grilling is impossible, grill the vegetables indoors under a high heat until lightly charred.

For the grilled vegetables:
1–2 potatoes, unpeeled and whole
1 red sweet pepper (capsicum), thickly sliced
1 eggplant (aubergine), sliced
2–3 zucchini (courgettes), thickly sliced lengthwise
juice from 1–2 lemons
extra virgin olive oil as desired
3 garlic cloves, coarsely chopped
½–1 teaspoon thyme
salt and pepper

For the soup:
5 garlic cloves, coarsely chopped
2 tablespoons extra virgin olive oil
7 oz. (200 g) cooked or tinned chickpeas, drained
4–5 in. (10–12 cm) sprig fresh rosemary
12 oz. (375 g) fresh or tinned tomatoes, chopped
4 cups (1¾ imp. pints, 1 litre) vegetable broth (see p. 15)
6 oz. (185 g) orzo or similar-shaped pasta
2–3 tablespoons pesto (see p. 16)
2 oz. (60 g) Parmesan cheese, freshly grated
extra virgin olive oil for drizzling, if desired

Prepare the vegetables: boil the potatoes until *al dente*, or not quite tender. Drain, and when just cool enough to handle, slice thickly. Drizzle the hot potato slices with about one-third of the lemon juice, olive oil, garlic, and thyme and leave to marinate for at least 30 minutes.

In a separate shallow flat pan or dish, place the red sweet pepper, eggplant, and zucchini, and drizzle with remaining lemon juice, olive oil, garlic, and thyme. Season with salt and pepper and leave to marinate for at least 30 minutes (potatoes and vegetables can marinate nicely for up to 12 hours, or overnight).

Remove vegetables from their marinade, reserving the lemon and olive oil mixture, and grill the vegetables over an open flame or under a high heat until lightly charred. Remove from heat and return to the marinade. Leave them in the marinade while you prepare the rest of the soup. (This can all be done a day ahead.)

Lightly sauté the garlic in the olive oil until just golden, then stir in the chickpeas and cook for a 1–2 minutes. Add the rosemary sprig, tomatoes, bouillon, orzo, and grilled vegetables, and cook until the pastina is *al dente*. The soup will become very thick.

Stir the pesto into the soup and serve each bowlful sprinkled with the Parmesan cheese. Drizzle with a little extra olive oil if desired.

SERVES 4–6

Broccoli and Pastina in Garlic Broth

A light and zesty soup, fragrant with sweetly simmered garlic, studded with crunchy-tender broccoli and tiny pasta shapes.

2 large heads garlic, cloves separated and peeled
4 cups (1¾ imp. pints, 1 litre) vegetable broth (see p. 15)
3 oz. (225 g) pastina, such as stelline, alphabets, orzo, acini de pepe, etc.
1 large bunch broccoli, cut into bite-sized florets and chunks of peeled stem
freshly grated Parmesan cheese to serve
extra virgin olive oil to serve
salt and freshly ground black pepper, to taste

Simmer the whole garlic cloves in the broth until tender (about 20 minutes). Add the pastina and cook for 2 minutes or so, then add the broccoli and continue cooking until both pasta and broccoli are *al dente*.

Serve hot, each portion sprinkled with Parmesan cheese and olive oil (if desired), and salt and freshly ground black pepper.

SERVES 4–6

RIGHT ◆ *Mediterranean Roasted Vegetable Soup–Stew*

Italian Soup of Pumpkin, Beans, and Orzo

Earthy pumpkin and red beans combine with small, tender orzo for a risotto-like pasta dish.

3 garlic cloves, chopped

1½ tablespoons extra virgin olive oil

1 lb (500 g) pumpkin, peeled and diced

3 cups (24 fl. oz., 750 ml) vegetable broth (see p. 15)

8 fl. oz. (250 ml) tomato purée (passata)

4 oz. (125 g) orzo or similar pasta

14 oz. (435 g) cooked or drained tinned kidney beans

6–8 oz. (185–250 g) chard (silver beet) or spinach, coarsely chopped or thinly sliced

salt, freshly ground black pepper, and dried oregano, to taste

freshly grated Parmesan cheese to serve

Lightly sauté the garlic in the olive oil for just a moment; add the pumpkin and turn in the garlic and oil to coat.

Pour in the broth and tomato purée, then cover and cook over medium heat until the squash or pumpkin is almost tender. Add the pasta and continue cooking for another 10–15 minutes until *al dente.*

Add the kidney beans and chard or spinach, and cook until chard or spinach is bright green and just tender.

Season with salt, freshly ground black pepper, and oregano, and serve immediately, accompanied by grated Parmesan cheese.

SERVES 4–6

BELOW ♦ *Italian Soup of Pumpkin, Beans, and Orzo*

Brown Lentil, Red Bean, Broccoli, and Pasta Shell Stew

This is a hearty soup–stew in the robust minestrone style. For a main course, omit the grated cheese and serve each portion of soup–stew ladled over a slab of milk-white cheese to melt in; as you eat the soup, each spoonful will yield a tiny bit of the rich cheese as well.
Leftovers are delicious reheated; I usually add a fresh lashing of chopped garlic, and sometimes give it a spicy shake of hot chili pepper sauce or cayenne pepper.

9 oz. (280 g) Puy lentils, or other brown or green lentils
4 cups (1¾ imp. pints, 1 litre) vegetable broth (see p. 15)
3 oz. (90 g) tomato paste (purée)
8 oz. (250 g) ripe tomatoes, diced, or 14-oz. (435-g) tin chopped tomatoes
1 bunch broccoli or spinach, cut into bite-sized pieces
14 oz. (435 g) cooked or tinned borlotti or red kidney beans, drained
6 oz. (185 g) pasta shells or other medium to large macaroni shapes
large pinch of each of dried thyme, sage, rosemary, and mixed herbs
4 garlic cloves, chopped
8 oz. (250 g) cheese of choice, grated
salt and freshly ground black pepper, to taste
3 tablespoons extra virgin olive oil, or to taste
3 tablespoons chopped fresh parsley

Cook the lentils in the broth until just tender (about an hour).

Add the tomato paste, tomatoes, broccoli or spinach, beans, pasta, herbs, and half the garlic. Continue cooking until the pasta is *al dente*.

Gently stir in the remaining garlic, cheese, salt, if needed, and black pepper.

Serve immediately, each portion sprinkled with olive oil and parsley.

VARIATION
Use an assortment of different types of beans, Calabrian style: combine borlotti, cannellini (white kidney) beans, fava (broad) beans, and chickpeas. Decrease the amount of lentils to a small handful, and substitute cabbage for the broccoli or spinach. Calabrians generally use spaghetti broken into thirds in place of macaroni and serve the hefty soup sprinkled with olive oil and parsley, omitting the cheese stirred into the above recipe.

SERVES 6

Tomato and Garlic Broth with Acini de Pepe, from an Italian Countryside Summer

Acini de pepe means grains of black peppercorns. They are all exactly the same size and have a delightful consistency, slithering down your throat as you swallow your soup. If acini de pepe are not available, use orzo, stelline, or other very small pasta.

1 onion, chopped
3 garlic cloves, chopped
2 teaspoons fresh thyme or ½ teaspoon dried thyme
1 carrot, diced
2–3 tablespoons extra virgin olive oil
4–5 fresh or tinned tomatoes, coarsely chopped
8 fl. oz. (250 ml) tomato juice, or about half that amount of tomato purée (passata)
3 cups (24 fl. oz., 750 ml) vegetable broth (see p. 15)
4–6 oz. (125–185 g) ancini de pepe or other small, firm-textured pasta
freshly grated Parmesan cheese to serve

Sauté the onion, garlic, thyme, and carrot in the olive oil until softened and lightly golden. Add the tomatoes and continue cooking for 3–5 minutes.

Add the tomato juice, broth, and pasta. Bring to the boil, then reduce the heat and simmer until the pasta is tender (about 10 minutes) depending on the pasta you choose. Be careful not to overcook the pasta.

Serve immediately, offering freshly grated Parmesan cheese separately.

SERVES 4

Pasta e Fagioli alla Toscana (Tuscan Soup of Puréed Beans with Pasta)

Tuscany is known in Italy as the land of bean-eaters because of their consumption of hearty legume dishes such as this one. It makes a good main course, and leftovers just seem to get better for several days, as you simmer in whatever is languishing in your refrigerator: zucchini (courgettes), spinach, etc., turning the potful into a minestrone. Since the pasta is apt to disintegrate when the leftover soup is reheated, you will probably want to add more, as you add more vegetables, broth, and seasonings.

3–5 garlic cloves, chopped
1½ tablespoons extra virgin olive oil
8 fresh or tinned tomatoes, diced
2 teaspoons chopped fresh rosemary leaves
14 oz. (435 g) cooked or drained tinned beans (either cannellini (white kidney) beans or chickpeas)
4 fl. oz. (125 ml) tomato purée (passata) or tomato juice
4 cups (1¾ imp. pints, 1 litre) vegetable broth (see p. 15)
pinch of red chili pepper flakes
salt and freshly ground black pepper, to taste
3–4 oz. (90–125 g) flat pasta ribbons or medium sized pasta shapes

Lightly sauté the garlic in 1 tablespoon of the olive oil. When it begins to color, add the tomatoes and rosemary. Cook over a high heat for 5–10 minutes, until sauce-like.

Mash the beans coarsely, leaving some whole, in a food processor or by using a potato masher. Add the beans to the sauce, then add the tomato purée, broth, red chili pepper flakes, salt if needed, black pepper, and pasta. Cook over medium heat until the pasta is tender (this will depend upon the type of pasta you choose).

Serve immediately, drizzling the remaining olive oil over each portion.

SERVES 4

RIGHT ◆ *Macaroni with Red Beans and Tomatoes*

Spicy Spanish Cabbage and Tomato Soup with Capellini

Shredded cabbage bubbles away in a mildly chili pepper-flavored tomato broth, enriched with a handful of thin capellini — such humble ingredients are transformed into an outstanding soup.

1 onion, coarsely chopped
6–8 garlic cloves, coarsely chopped
2 tablespoons extra virgin olive oil
2–3 teaspoons paprika, to taste
2–3 teaspoons mild chili pepper powder
½ teaspoon cumin
½ green or white cabbage, very thinly sliced
4–6 cups (1¾–2½ imp. pints, 1–1½ litres) vegetable broth (see p. 15)
1½ lb (750 g) ripe tomatoes, peeled, seeded, and diced, or 1½–2 14-oz. (435-g) tins chopped tomatoes
4 oz. (125 g) capellini or similar very fine pasta
2–3 tablespoons coarsely chopped fresh coriander leaves
lemon or lime wedges to serve

Lightly sauté the onion and garlic in the olive oil until softened; sprinkle in the paprika, chili pepper powder, and cumin and cook for a moment or two.

Add the cabbage, about two-thirds of the broth, and half the tomatoes. Bring to the boil, then reduce the heat and let it simmer for 1 hour, adding extra broth to replace any liquid that boils away. Add the remaining tomatoes and cook for another 30 minutes or so.

Meanwhile, cook the pasta until *al dente*, drain, and add to the soup.

Serve sprinkled with the coriander leaves and accompanied with wedges of lemon or lime to squeeze into the soup.

VARIATION
Instead of capellini, serve the spicy cabbage and tomato soup with small, chewy dumplings, such as spätzle (see p. 170).

SERVES 6

Macaroni with Red Beans and Tomatoes

Robust and homey, this makes a sustaining supper dish. You could include other vegetables if you like, such as chard (silver beet), cabbage, green beans, etc., but it is delicious as it is, with its small nuggets of onion, celery, and carrot. The bean broth forms the cooking liquid for the pasta, and once it is all cooked together it is thick and soupy. Serve with a generous sprinkling of any sharp cheese.

Dishes like this, based on beans and their cooking liquid, are great to have in your culinary repertoire. Tinned beans are fine in many recipes, but in ones like this where you need the cooking liquid as well, the liquid from the tin is too salty and metallic-tasting, so use fresh beans.

8 oz. (250 g) dried red kidney beans
1 onion, coarsely chopped
1 carrot, diced
2 celery stalks, chopped
3 garlic cloves, chopped
1 tablespoon chopped parsley (optional)
2 tablespoons extra virgin olive oil
10 fresh or tinned tomatoes, peeled and diced
8 fl. oz. (250 ml) tomato juice
½ vegetable bouillon (stock) cube
8 oz. (250 g) short macaroni
1 tablespoon tomato paste (purée)
1 teaspoon dried mixed herbs
salt and freshly ground black pepper, to taste
4 oz. (125 g) grated cheese, or to taste

Cook the beans until tender and leave to cool in their cooking liquid. Lightly sauté the onion, carrot, celery, garlic, and parsley (if using) in the olive oil until softened and lightly browned.

Ladle in the beans and 2 cups (16 fl. oz., 500 ml) of their cooking liquid, the tomatoes, tomato juice, bouillon cube, and macaroni and bring to the boil. Cook over medium heat for about 5–7 minutes, stirring carefully so as not to break up pasta.

Cover and leave to stand for a few minutes to let the pasta absorb the liquid and plump up. If the mixture seems too dry, add more bean cooking liquid or tomato juice.

Stir in the tomato paste, mixed herbs, salt and pepper. Serve immediately, each portion sprinkled with cheese.

SERVES 4–6

Pasta Stew with Cannellini Beans and Black Olive Sauce

Olive paste, oily, pungent, and black, adds a touch of piquancy to this soup–stew of beans and pasta. If olive paste is unavailable, make your own by mincing pitted Mediterranean-style black olives in a food processor and adding enough olive oil to make a smooth paste.

6 oz. (185 g) ditalini or other short macaroni
1 onion, thinly sliced
1 small to medium carrot, diced
2 garlic cloves, coarsely chopped
8 oz. (250 g) cooked or drained tinned cannellini
  (white kidney) beans
1½ lb (750 g) ripe tomatoes, peeled and diced,
  or 1½ 14-oz. (435-g) tins chopped tomatoes
2 tablespoons chopped fresh parsley
2 cups (16 fl. oz., 500 ml) vegetable broth
  (see p. 15)
salt and freshly ground black pepper, to taste

Olive Sauce
1 large clove garlic, chopped
1 teaspoon chopped fresh rosemary
1 tablespoon olive paste
3 tablespoons extra virgin olive oil

Cook the pasta until *al dente*. Drain and rinse with cold water then set aside.

Lightly sauté the onion, carrot, and garlic until softened; add the beans, tomatoes, parsley, and broth and simmer for 5–10 minutes.

Meanwhile, mix all the ingredients for the olive sauce together. (This may be made in advance and stored in the refrigerator for up to a month.)

Add the pasta to the stew, reheat gently, and serve each portion garnished with the olive sauce.

VARIATION
Cannellini Bean and Orzo Stew: Small, rice-shaped orzo is very good in this bean and pasta dish. Serve with a drizzle of lemon juice or wine vinegar, a sprinkling of oregano and chopped raw garlic, instead of olive sauce.

SERVES 4–6

Middle Eastern Cinnamon-scented Egg and Lemon Soup with Zucchini and Thin Pasta

Thickening simple broths with a mixture of eggs beaten with lemon juice is a distinctively Middle Eastern technique, with variations throughout the region. Adding a little cinnamon is a culinary souvenir of Egypt, and its sweet scent is particularly nice with the tangy lemon and rich egg. Diced zucchini (courgettes) add a juicy, chunky vegetable texture to the soup.

4 cups (1¾ imp. pints, 1 litre) vegetable broth
  (see p. 15)
1 lb (500 g) zucchini (courgettes), diced or sliced
4 garlic cloves, coarsely chopped
1 cinnamon stick
handful of thin pasta strands (spaghetti, capellini,
  etc.), broken into short lengths
salt and cayenne pepper, to taste
2 eggs, lightly beaten
juice of 1–2 lemons, to taste
fresh coriander leaves for garnish

Combine the stock, zucchini, garlic, cinnamon, and pasta in a pan. Bring to the boil and cook until the pasta is *al dente* and the zucchini are tender. Season with salt and cayenne pepper.

Mix the beaten eggs with the lemon juice, then add a ladleful of hot soup and stir well to combine. Add another ladleful of soup, stirring well to make a creamy mixture rather than scrambled egg.

Off the heat, stir the egg and lemon mixture into the hot soup, then return the pan to the stove and cook over medium heat until it begins to thicken.

Serve immediately, garnished with coriander leaves.

SERVES 4–6

RIGHT ♦ *Pasta Stew with Cannellini Beans and Black Olive Sauce*

African Spicy Peanut Soup–Stew with Noodles

This African-inspired soup–stew is a version of one filled with vegetables, chilies, and peanuts that I make at least once a month. I usually fling open the refrigerator to see what vegetables are languishing there, ready to be simmered in this spicy soup. But recently, when it was time to serve the soup, I added handfuls of cooked noodles — no doubt a result of testing recipes for this book. I have since prepared this soup using couscous or thin rice noodles.
As a young friend from Ethiopia, Eyob, exclaimed as he lifted the first spoonful to his lips: 'It tastes, it actually tastes! Nothing I have eaten since I've been here could I taste!' There was a smile on his face.

4 shallots or 1 onion, chopped
3 garlic cloves, chopped
2 tablespoons vegetable oil
1 bay leaf
1 teaspoon paprika
½ teaspoon curry powder, or to taste
½ teaspoon cumin, or to taste
14 oz. (435 g) fresh or tinned tomatoes, diced
2½ cups (1 imp. pint, 600 ml) vegetable broth
 (see p. 15)
2–3 dried hot red chili peppers, left whole, or
 several generous shakes of dried red chili flakes
½ carrot, diced
¼ small to medium white or green cabbage, thinly
 sliced or coarsely chopped
handful of fresh or frozen green beans, cut into
 bite-sized lengths
2 oz. (60 g) fresh or frozen spinach, chopped
4–6 heaped tablespoons peanut butter, preferably
 unsweetened and chunky
juice of 1 lemon, or to taste
several tablespoons of yogurt, or to taste
salt and freshly ground black pepper, to taste
4 oz. (125 g) Chinese noodles (or rice noodles)
celery leaves and/or fresh coriander leaves
4 tablespoons crushed peanuts
hot pepper sauce
lemon wedges

Lightly sauté the shallots or onion and garlic in the oil until softened; add the bay leaf, paprika, curry powder, and cumin and cook for a moment. Add the tomatoes, broth, chilies, carrot, and cabbage, then bring to the boil. Reduce the heat and simmer until the vegetables are very soft (at least 30 minutes). Add the green beans and spinach and continue cooking for at least 20 minutes, until all the vegetables are soft. Stir in the peanut butter until melted; add the lemon juice, yogurt, salt, and black pepper. Add more curry powder or cumin if desired.

Cook the noodles until tender. Rinse with cold water and drain.

To serve, ladle the soup–stew over the noodles. Garnish with celery leaves and/or coriander leaves, sprinkle with the crushed peanuts, and offer hot pepper sauce and lemon wedges separately.

SERVES 4–6

Provençal Garlic Soup

Sweet garlic broth, scented with sage, simmered with thin pasta, then enriched with egg and Parmesan cheese, makes an invigorating yet simply prepared soup.

2 heads garlic, cloves separated and peeled
4 cups (1¾ imp. pints, 1 litre) vegetable broth
 (see p. 15)
1 teaspoon sage leaves, lightly crumbled if dried,
 chopped if fresh
tiny pinch of cayenne pepper
4 nests (about 3–4 oz. (90–125 g)) very thin pasta,
 broken up a little
2 eggs, lightly beaten
2 oz. (60 g) Parmesan cheese, freshly grated

Put garlic cloves, broth, sage and cayenne pepper in a pan and bring to the boil. Reduce the heat and simmer for about 20 minutes. Halfway through the cooking add the pasta, separating it into strands as it softens, and continue cooking until both pasta and garlic are tender.

Combine the eggs with the Parmesan cheese. Ladle a little hot broth into the egg mixture, stir well; repeat. Off the heat, stir this mixture into the hot broth, letting it become creamy rather than letting the egg mixture cook. Return to the heat and cook, stirring, over low to medium heat until the soup thickens slightly. Serve immediately.

SERVES 4

Chickpea and Tagliatelle Soup

*Simple fare from Italy's deep south, this broth is filled with
garlic-and-onion-sautéed chickpeas and tender tagliatelle.*

2 small to medium onions, chopped
3 garlic cloves, chopped
1 small carrot, chopped
1 tablespoon chopped fresh parsley
2 tablespoons extra virgin olive oil
salt and freshly ground black pepper
14 oz. (435 g) cooked or tinned chickpeas, drained
4 cups (1¾ imp. pints, 1 litre) vegetable broth (p. 15)
6 oz. (185 g) fresh or dried tagliatelle

Lightly sauté the onions, garlic, carrot, and parsley in the
olive oil until the onions are softened. Season with salt
and black pepper; add the chickpeas and cook for a few
minutes. Add the broth and bring to the boil; simmer for
10 minutes or until well flavored. Taste for seasoning.

Meanwhile, cook the pasta until *al dente;* drain. Add
to the soup and serve.

VARIATIONS
**Chickpea and Tagliatelle Soup with Tomatoes and
Rosemary:** Add 1 lb (500 g) ripe chopped tomatoes, or
14-oz. (435-g) tin chopped tomatoes to the recipe above,
along with 1½–2 teaspoons chopped fresh rosemary.
Pasta e Ceci alla Leccese: From Lecce (Apulia) comes
this pasta and chickpea soup which is strikingly different
from others in that half the pasta is fried while the other
half is boiled. It gives an unusual texture and richness to
the soup.

Prepare the basic soup recipe but use fresh tagliatelle
and increase the amount to 8 oz. (250 g). Fry half of it
until lightly golden, then drain on absorbent paper
towels. Add the fried pasta to the soup at the end of its
cooking time and cook for 1–3 minutes before serving.
Season with hot red chili pepper flakes, and if the pasta
has not been fried in olive oil, anoint the soup with a
drizzle of olive oil before serving.

SERVES 4

ABOVE ♦ *Chickpea and Tagliatelle Soup*

Cold Pasta Dishes

Cold pasta served with a raw
or quickly cooked sauce and garnished with fresh vegetables can be
one of the most refreshing dishes imaginable. The supple, cool noodles should contrast with the vivacious
flavors and crisp textures they are paired with: strong-flavored ingredients such as garlic, olive or sesame oil,
onions, tomatoes, crisp vegetables, nuts, herbs,
and tangy cheeses.

◆ ◆ ◆

The important thing about cold pasta
is that it retain its freshness don't be tempted to turn it into the pasta-salad rubbish bin that some restaurants
and recipes do. Cold pasta should never be chilled to numbness, though a nicely chilled
sauce can be an exciting counterpoint to freshly cooked hot pasta. Since many Far Eastern
pasta dishes are enjoyed cold as well, do refer to that chapter (pp. 136–151)
for additional recipes.

♦ ♦ ♦

Penne with Red Sweet Peppers, Feta, and Mint

Like goat cheese, slightly creamy, pungent, and salty feta cheese combines brilliantly with bland pasta. Red sweet peppers (capsicum) and garlic, lemon, and mint, all amplify the Mediterranean flavor focus.

3 red sweet peppers (capsicums)
2 garlic cloves, chopped
4 oz. (125 g) feta cheese, crumbled
3 tablespoons extra virgin olive oil
12 oz. (375 g) penne (pasta quills)
juice of 1 lemon, or to taste
coarsely ground black pepper, to taste
2 sprigs fresh mint

Roast the red sweet peppers as described on page 19, then cut into bite-sized pieces.

Combine the roasted red sweet peppers with the garlic, feta cheese, and olive oil.

Cook the pasta until *al dente*; drain, then toss with the pepper and feta cheese mixture. Season with the lemon juice and black pepper, and serve either hot or cold, garnished with the mint.

VARIATION

Penne with Black Olives, Feta, and Parsley: Substitute black Kalamata or oil-cured olives, pitted and quartered, for the grilled red sweet peppers (capsicum) and use chopped parsley instead of, or in addition to, the mint. Proceed as above.

SERVES 4

Pasta Shells and Broccoli with Spicy–Tangy Tahini Dressing

Sesame-rich tahini makes a delicious and healthy dressing for this pasta and broccoli salad.

12 oz. (375 g) pasta shells
1 large bunch broccoli, cut into bite-sized pieces
1 dried hot red chili pepper, crumbled
6 garlic cloves, coarsely chopped
3 tablespoons extra virgin olive oil
½ cup (4 fl. oz., 125 ml) tahini, mashed with a fork to smooth any lumps
1 teaspoon cumin
juice of 1 lemon, plus extra lemon wedges to serve
pinch of turmeric or curry powder
salt and freshly ground black pepper, to taste

Cook the pasta until half-done. Add the broccoli and continue cooking until the pasta and broccoli are both *al dente*; drain.

Heat the red chili pepper and half the garlic in the olive oil. Toss the pasta and broccoli in this mixture and set aside to cool.

Mix the remaining garlic with the tahini, cumin, lemon juice, turmeric or curry powder, salt, and black pepper, and enough water to make a paste about the consistency of thick cream.

Just before serving, combine the pasta and broccoli with the tahini sauce. Serve with lemon wedges.

SERVES 4

PREVIOUS PAGE ◆ *Pasta Shells and Broccoli with Spicy–Tangy Tahini Dressing (left) and Penne with Red Sweet Peppers, Feta, and Mint (right)*
RIGHT ◆ *Spicy Fragrant East–West Noodles*

Spicy Fragrant East–West Noodles

3 tablespoons fermented black beans, rinsed
  and drained
3 garlic cloves, chopped
grated rind of ½ orange or 1 tangerine
2–3 dried hot red chili peppers, crumbled
⅓ cup (3 fl. oz., 90 ml) vegetable oil
3 tablespoons toasted sesame oil
12 oz. (375 g) Chinese egg noodles or Italian
  vermicelli
3–4 tablespoons chopped fresh coriander leaves
½ cucumber, diced or coarsely chopped
2 to 3 tablespoons crushed or coarsely chopped
  peanuts or toasted almonds
2–3 scallions (spring onions), thinly sliced
soy sauce to taste

Gently heat the black beans, garlic, orange or tangerine rind, and red chili peppers in the vegetable oil. Do not let the garlic brown or let the mixture boil. Leave to cool, then mix with the toasted sesame oil. This will make more oil than you need for this recipe, but it will keep for months in a well-sealed jar and makes a good flavoring addition for a variety of dishes, especially those with a Far-Eastern accent.

Cook the noodles until *al dente;* drain and rinse with cold water, then drain again.

When ready to serve, toss the pasta with some of the flavored oil, then garnish with coriander leaves, cucumber, peanuts or almonds, and scallions, and sprinkle with soy sauce.

SERVES 4

Summer-afternoon Pasta with Tomatoes, Mozzarella, and Basil

Cool and refreshing for a summer lunch on a terrace in Tuscany, or in your own garden.

12 oz. (375 g) large pasta shells, or gnocchi shapes
6-oz. (185-g) jar peperoncini (Greek or Italian mildly spicy pickled peppers), drained
10–12 ripe sweet red tomatoes, diced, or use half fresh and half tinned
3 tablespoons extra virgin olive oil, or to taste
1 tablespoon red wine vinegar or sherry vinegar
large pinch of dried thyme, crumbled
large pinch of dried mint, crumbled
salt and cayenne pepper or hot red chili pepper flakes, to taste
4 oz. (125 g) mozzarella cheese, diced
handful of fresh basil leaves, thinly sliced

Cook the pasta until *al dente*. Drain and combine with the peperoncini, tomatoes, olive oil, vinegar, thyme, and mint. Leave to cool.

When cool, season with salt and cayenne pepper or red chili pepper flakes, then add the cheese and basil and chill until ready to serve.

SERVES 4

Garlic-and-olive-oil-scented Macaroni Salad with Tomatoes, Goat Cheese, and Basil

8–10 ripe tomatoes, diced
1 tablespoon balsamic or red wine vinegar, or to taste
salt and freshly ground black pepper, to taste
12 oz. (375 g) elbow pasta or lumachine
3 tablespoons extra virgin olive oil
3 garlic cloves, chopped
handful of fresh basil leaves, coarsely chopped
4 oz. (125 g) goat cheese, crumbled

Combine the tomatoes with the vinegar and salt and leave to stand while you cook the pasta until *al dente*.

Drain the pasta and toss with the olive oil and garlic.

When the pasta is warm but not hot, combine with the tomato mixture. Leave to cool completely and toss with the basil. Serve each portion topped with the crumbled goat cheese and black pepper to taste.

SERVES 4

Noodles with Coriander, Mint Raita, and Cucumber

A cool, green dressing that smells of sweet mint and spicy ginger, yet delivers a chili pepper wallop. Serve topped with a handful of thinly sliced coriander and mint leaves, and a scattering of crunchy chopped cucumber.

2 garlic cloves, finely chopped
1 fresh green chili pepper, or to taste, chopped
2 teaspoons chopped fresh ginger root
large bunch of fresh mint leaves, thinly sliced
large bunch of fresh coriander, thinly sliced
2 cups (16 fl. oz., 500 ml) Greek-style yogurt
salt to taste
12 oz. (375 g) spaghetti or dried Chinese egg noodles
several tablespoons of extra virgin olive oil
juice of ½ lemon, or to taste
¼–½ cucumber, coarsely chopped or finely diced, and drained of excess liquid

Combine the garlic, green chili pepper, ginger root, mint, and coriander, reserving a small handful of mint and coriander for garnish, and blend into a purée in a blender or food processor. Add the yogurt and blend into a pale green mixture. Season with salt and chill until ready to use (this may be made several days in advance).

Cook the spaghetti or noodles until *al dente*; drain and toss with olive oil to taste. Combine the pasta with the yogurt mixture, then season with the lemon juice.

Serve topped with a scattering of the reserved chopped coriander and mint and the cucumber.

SERVES 4–6

RIGHT ♦ *Summer-afternoon Pasta with Tomatoes, Mozzarella, and Basil*

Fourth of July Macaroni Salad

Before the advent of pasta salad, macaroni salad was the only cold pasta dish Americans knew. Seldom was there a gathering without a big bowlful; growing up I couldn't imagine a Fourth of July picnic without it. It consisted of macaroni bound together in a mayonnaise dressing, seasoned with onions, celery, hard-boiled egg, chopped sweet gherkins, diced tomato, etc. As tastes grew more sophisticated, macaroni salads disappeared in favor of pasta salads with pesto, sun-dried tomatoes, etc. But macaroni salad can be really good, and it is delicious any day of the year, not just the Fourth of July.

12 oz. (375 g) small to medium pasta shape of choice
3–4 oz. (90–125 g) fresh and blanched, or frozen, peas
4–6 heaped tablespoons mayonnaise, or to taste
1 tablespoon mustard of choice
1–2 celery stalks, plus leaves, chopped
½–1 small onion or 2 scallions (spring onions), chopped
1–2 hard-boiled eggs, quartered
6–8 pimiento-stuffed green olives, halved, or pickled cucumbers, such as gherkins or the French cornichons, coarsely chopped
few drops of vinegar or lemon juice
salt, freshly ground black pepper, and paprika, to taste
2 tablespoons chopped fresh parsley

Cook the pasta until *al dente*, adding the peas at the last minute; drain and rinse in cold water. Drain well again.

Combine the pasta and peas with all the remaining ingredients. Taste for seasoning.

Note: This is even better if it is left for a while for the flavors to blend. Store it in the refrigerator, as mayonnaise can quickly go off, even at room temperature.

SERVES 4

Aunt Estelle's Napa Cabbage Salad with Crunchy Noodles and Nuts

This unusual salad is prepared from Ramen-type noodles, the near-instant noodles that come in individual portions with their own soup, and are quickly boiled for a light lunch or snack. Here, however, they are browned until crisp rather than boiled. The crunchy noodles are then tossed, along with nuts, into a salad of Napa cabbage (Chinese leaves) with a sweet and savory dressing.

The recipe is courtesy of my Aunt Estelle, who is more glamorous than kitchen-bound but nonetheless often amazes me by waltzing into her kitchen and effortlessly whipping up something unusual and outstanding. The salad needs to be served immediately upon assembling, but the various components can be prepared up to two days in advance and put together when ready to be served.

1 large head Napa cabbage (Chinese leaves), including stalks and core, base trimmed, leaves coarsely chopped
6 scallions (spring onions), thinly sliced
1 packet Ramen-type noodles, coarsely crushed while still in the packet (reserve seasoning)
2 oz. (60 g) butter
3 tablespoons sesame seeds
2 oz. (60 g) slivered almonds or roasted peanuts, coarsely chopped
2 tablespoons chopped fresh ginger root
3 tablespoons soy sauce
⅓ cup (3 fl. oz., 90 ml) vegetable oil
2 tablespoons sesame oil
¼ cup (2 fl. oz., 60 ml) rice vinegar
3 oz. (90 g) sugar
salt and freshly ground black pepper, to taste
2–3 tablespoons fresh coriander leaves

Mix together the Napa cabbage and scallions; set aside.

Brown the noodles in the butter, together with sesame seeds, nuts, and seasoning powder from packet. When crunchy and deliciously browned (about 5–8 minutes) remove from the heat.

Make the dressing by combining the ginger root, soy sauce, vegetable oil, sesame oil, rice vinegar, and sugar. Mix well, then season with salt and black pepper. The dressing will seem sweet, but it works well with the other ingredients.

Just before serving, toss the Napa cabbage and scallions with the dressing, then top with a generous sprinkling of seeds, nuts, crispy noodles, and fresh coriander leaves.

SERVES 4

Capellini with Beet Relish, Broccoli, and Blue Cheese

4 medium to large beets (beetroot), cooked but unvinegared
1 small to medium onion, chopped
1 tablespoon wine vinegar
sugar, salt, freshly ground black pepper, and dried mixed herbs, to taste
2 tablespoons oil of choice
12 oz. (375 g) capellini
2 bunches broccoli, cut into florets, the stalks peeled and sliced
1 tablespoon extra virgin olive oil
4½ oz. (140 g) blue cheese, such as a very ripe Danish blue, Roquefort, or Gorgonzola, crumbled into large pieces

Prepare the relish by dicing the beets and combining with the onion. Dress with the vinegar, a generous sprinkling of sugar, salt, black pepper, mixed herbs, and the oil. Set aside for at least 15 minutes.

Cook the capellini until half-done, then add the broccoli and continue cooking until capellini and broccoli are both tender. Drain and dress with the olive oil, salt, and black pepper. Cool to room temperature or slightly warmer.

Serve each portion of pasta and broccoli topped with a spoonful or two of the relish, including some of the marinade, and the nuggets of cheese.

SERVES 4

LEFT ♦ *Fourth of July Macaroni Salad*

Fusilli Salad with Zucchini, Sun-dried Tomatoes, and Rosemary

12 oz. (375 g) fusilli or other twisty pasta
4 small to medium zucchini (courgettes), cut into
    bite-sized pieces
1–2 garlic cloves, chopped
2 teaspoons chopped fresh rosemary leaves
3 tablespoons extra virgin olive oil
10 oil-marinated sun-dried tomatoes, drained and
    coarsely chopped
salt and freshly ground black pepper, to taste
dash of red wine vinegar (optional)

Boil the pasta until half-cooked, then add the zucchini and continue cooking until both are *al dente;* drain.

Toss with the garlic, rosemary, olive oil, and sun-dried tomatoes; leave to cool. Season before serving with salt, black pepper, and the red wine vinegar if desired.

SERVES 4

BELOW ♦ *Fusilli Salad with Zucchini, Sun-dried Tomatoes, and Rosemary*

Pasta Shells with Zucchini and Tomato–Olive Relish

6–8 fresh or tinned tomatoes, chopped
10–15 oil-cured black Mediterranean olives, such as
    Kalamata or Niçoise, pitted and diced
2 tablespoons extra virgin olive oil
2 teaspoons red wine vinegar
12 oz. (375 g) pasta shells (or elbows, ditalini, or
    other short macaroni)
2 zucchini (courgettes), diced
salt and freshly ground black pepper, to taste
2 tablespoons chopped fresh parsley

Combine the tomatoes, olives, oil, and vinegar; set aside. Cook the pasta until almost *al dente.* Add the zucchini and continue cooking until both are *al dente;* drain.

Toss the hot pasta and zucchini with the cool tomato mixture. Add salt and black pepper, sprinkle with the chopped parsley, and serve at room temperature.

SERVES 4

RIGHT ♦ *Pasta Shells with Zucchini and Tomato–Olive Relish*

Chinese Peanut Butter-dressed Noodle Salad with Red Cabbage and Bean Sprouts

Red cabbage, cucumber, carrot, and bean sprouts all provide the fresh crunch, chilied peanut sauce the spicy counterpoint, and bland Chinese noodles the base for the dish. Perfect for an informal summer lunch or buffet, and nice for a picnic, too.

3 garlic cloves, finely chopped
4 heaped tablespoons peanut butter
1–2 teaspoons chopped fresh ginger root
½ fresh hot red chili pepper, chopped, or cayenne pepper, to taste
2 tablespoons lemon juice
2 tablespoons sugar
1–2 tablespoons soy sauce, plus a little more to toss with the noodles
1 tablespoon sesame oil, plus a little more to toss with the noodles
¼ cup (2 fl. oz., 60 ml) water
1 lb (500 g) fresh Chinese noodles or 12 oz. (375 g) dried noodles
1 bunch scallions (spring onions), thinly sliced
4 oz. (125 g) bean sprouts
½ cucumber, diced
¼ red cabbage, diced or shredded
1 carrot, grated
2–3 tablespoons whole fresh coriander leaves

Combine the garlic, peanut butter, ginger root, red chili pepper or cayenne pepper, lemon juice, sugar, soy sauce, and the sesame oil in a blender (liquidizer) or food processor and process until smooth and thick.

Add the water slowly as the machine whirls, letting the mixture form a thickish sauce. Taste for seasoning; it should be sweet, tart, nutty, and quite spicy. Set aside.

Cook the noodles until *al dente*. Drain and rinse with cold water, then drain well again. Toss with a little sesame oil and soy sauce, then leave to cool.

Combine the cool noodles with the scallions, bean sprouts, cucumber, red cabbage, and carrot, then top with the peanut sauce.

Serve sprinkled with the coriander leaves.

SERVES 4–6

Farfalle with Multicolored Tomato Salad

Multicolored tomatoes are a delight, not only to the eye but to the tastebuds as well; each different shape and color has its own flavor, sweetness, and acidity. If you have a garden, grow as many types as you can; if not, seek out particularly tasty tomatoes and varied types. In addition to yellow and red ones, there are orange ones, variegated ones, and even a ripe green tomato that tastes luscious and sweet rather than overly tart, as unripe tomatoes normally do.
In the following recipe, if multicolored tomatoes are not available, use ordinary red ones.

12 oz. (375 g) green farfalle
3 garlic cloves, chopped
3 tablespoons extra virgin olive oil
5–6 ripe, sweet tomatoes, preferably a combination of red and yellow tomatoes, or a handful of tiny yellow and red cherry tomatoes
salt and freshly ground black pepper, to taste
pinch of sugar
balsamic vinegar to taste
several fresh basil leaves, rolled up and cut into thin strips

Cook the pasta until *al dente*. Drain and toss with the garlic and olive oil and leave to cool.

Dice the tomatoes and season with salt and black pepper, sugar, and balsamic vinegar.

Combine the cool pasta with the seasoned tomatoes and serve, sprinkled generously with basil.

SERVES 4

Cold Pasta with Broccoli, Sesame, and Soy

The combination of pasta, a crisp-tender vegetable such as broccoli, and a simple glistening of nutty sesame oil and salty soy sauce is far more delicious than any recipe this easy and uncomplicated deserves to be.

12 oz. (375 g) pasta of choice: chunky elbows, seashells, fettuccine, Chinese pasta, lasagne, etc.
10–12 oz. (310–375 g) broccoli, cut into bite-sized pieces
2–3 tablespoons toasted sesame oil, to taste
soy sauce to taste
1 clove garlic, chopped (optional)
2 tablespoons toasted sesame seeds
1 tablespoon coarsely chopped coriander leaves

Boil the pasta until half-cooked; add the broccoli and continue cooking until the pasta is *al dente* and the broccoli is crisp-tender.

Drain and rinse in cold water. When cool, dress in sesame oil and soy sauce, add the garlic if using, and sprinkle with the sesame seeds and coriander leaves.

VARIATION
Spicy Penne with Green Beans, Chinese Style: Substitute thin green beans, cut into bite-sized pieces, for the broccoli. Add a shake of hot chili pepper sauce, such as Tabasco, for extra zest.

SERVES 4

BELOW ♦ *Chinese Peanut Butter-dressed Noodle Salad with Red Cabbage and Bean Sprouts*

Roasted Garlic with Cumin–Eggplant and Capellini

This recipe appears in The Flavor of California *(Thorsons), but I thought it was worth including it in this collection for its distinctive and unusual character. With Middle Eastern rather than Italian flavors and perfumes, it is unexpectedly delicious.*

3 heads garlic, broken into cloves but left unpeeled, plus 2 cloves raw garlic, peeled and chopped
3–4 tablespoons extra virgin olive oil
salt and cayenne pepper, to taste
1 eggplant (aubergine), thinly sliced lengthwise
1–2 teaspoons cumin, or to taste
12 oz. (375 g) capellini
juice of ½ lemon
2 teaspoons chopped fresh coriander leaves or parsley

Place the whole unpeeled garlic cloves on a baking sheet (tray) in a single layer and sprinkle with 2 tablespoons of the olive oil and salt to taste. Roast in the oven at 350°F (180°C) for 30 minutes, then raise the heat to 400°F (200°C) for another 10 minutes.

Remove from the oven and, when cool enough to handle, remove the skins. Toss the cooked garlic flesh with the oil in which it has cooked, if any remains, and set aside.

Brush the eggplant slices with the remaining olive oil and sprinkle with about 1 teaspoon cumin. Broil (grill) until browned in spots and tender, then cut into matchstick pieces.

Cook the pasta until *al dente;* drain. Toss with the remaining olive oil and cumin, the roasted garlic flesh, and the eggplant. Season with salt, cayenne pepper, and the lemon juice. Add extra olive oil and cumin, if needed, and serve at room temperature, garnished with the coriander or parsley.

SERVES 4

Pacific Rim Pasta: Rice Noodles with Tomato–Chili Pepper Salsa

Tender rice noodles from the Far East, served cool with a spicy South-of-the-Border tomato and chili pepper salsa, drizzled with olive oil and ground cumin. A refreshing and sprightly dish for a sultry afternoon or evening.

1 packet (about 13 oz. (405 g)) rice noodles, about ⅛ in. (3mm) wide
12 oz. (375 g) ripe or tinned tomatoes, diced
3 tablespoons coarsely chopped fresh coriander leaves
3 garlic cloves, chopped
1–3 fresh green chili peppers, to taste, thinly sliced or chopped
½ teaspoon mild red chili pepper powder, or to taste
salt to taste
1 tablespoon extra virgin olive oil
squeeze of lemon juice
½ teaspoon cumin, or to taste

Cook the rice noodles until just tender; drain and rinse in cold water.

To make the salsa: combine the tomatoes with 2 tablespoons of the coriander, garlic, chili peppers, and chili pepper powder. Leave to marinate for at least 30 minutes.

Just before serving, combine the rice noodles with the salsa. Season with salt and serve drizzled with the olive oil and lemon juice, and sprinkled with the cumin and remaining coriander leaves.

SERVES 4–6

RIGHT ♦ *Roasted Garlic with Cumin–Eggplant and Cappellini*

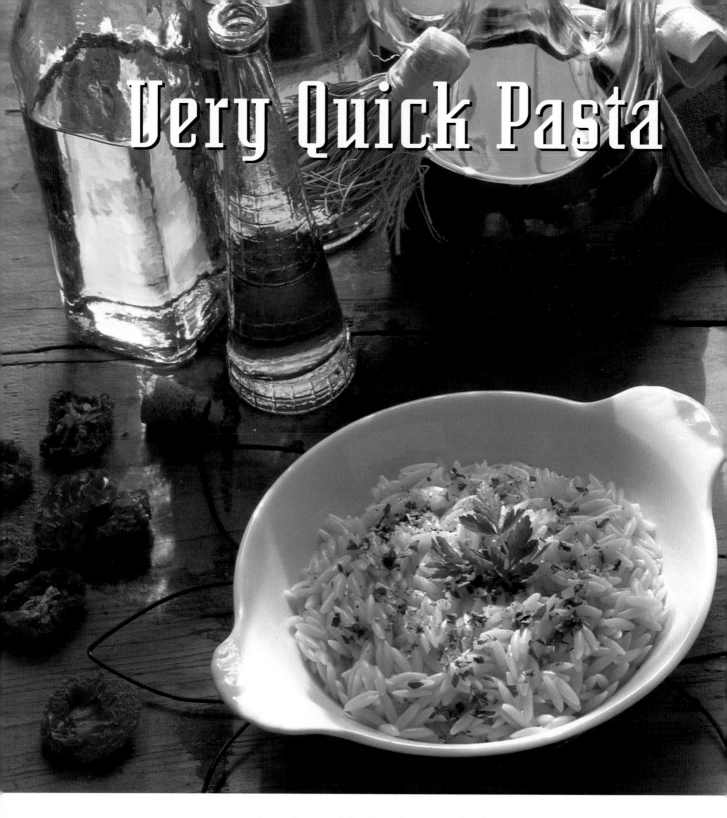

Very Quick Pasta

*A good part of the joy of pasta is the fact that
a welcoming plateful can be yours in a very short time, providing you have a few basic ingredients
on hand: olive oil, garlic, and something — almost anything — fresh. Fresh vegetables and herbs are the
stars here — a handful of blanched vegetables or fragrant herbs tossed in hot garlicky oil or butter
makes an almost instant and immensely satisfying dish. Purée it and you have a
different savory dish; lash it with cream, yet another.*

◆ ◆ ◆

Storecupboard specialties,
such as pesto, olive paste, sun-dried tomatoes, etc., multiply the variety of flavors
and recipes you have at your fingertips. These condiments add intense, concentrated flavor
to quickly prepared dishes, and can sit on your kitchen shelf almost
indefinitely awaiting the pleasures of
your table.

♦ ♦ ♦

Broth-cooked Orzo with Lemon and Parsley

Cooking pasta in broth gives extra flavor. The garlic is optional — it really is a nice dish without it, but I cannot resist its lure.

4 cups (1¾ imp. pints, 1 litre) vegetable broth (see p. 15)
12 oz. (375 g) orzo or other very small pasta
1 tablespoon extra virgin olive oil
1–2 garlic cloves, finely chopped
juice of 1–2 lemons, to taste
1 oz. (30 g) fresh parsley, chopped
salt and freshly ground black pepper, to taste

Bring the broth to the boil; add the pasta and cook until *al dente*. Drain the pasta and reserve the broth for another use.

Toss the orzo with the olive oil and garlic, then season with the lemon juice, parsley, salt, and black pepper. Serve immediately.

SERVES 4

Fettuccine with a Confetti of Vegetables and Garlic–Mint Sauce

2 celery stalks, cut into matchsticks
2 carrots, cut into matchsticks
12 oz. (375 g) fresh fettuccine
8 garlic cloves, coarsely chopped
½ cup (4 fl. oz., 125 ml) extra virgin olive oil
3–4 tablespoons coarsely chopped fresh mint leaves
salt and freshly ground black pepper, to taste

Place the celery and carrots in a large pan of water, bring to the boil, then add the fettuccine and salt. Cook until *al dente* (3–4 minutes); drain.

Meanwhile, warm the garlic in the olive oil until fragrant and slightly golden, then remove from the heat and add the mint leaves, pepper, and extra salt to taste.

Toss the pasta and vegetables with the garlic–mint sauce and serve immediately.

SERVES 4

Lumachine with Sun-dried Tomatoes

Strips of sun-dried tomato soften in the boiling water as the pasta cooks; simply buttered and seasoned with garlic and thyme, this makes a pleasant and easy meal.

12 oz. (375 g) lumachine (shells), farfalle (butterflies) or elbow-shaped pasta
10–15 sun-dried tomatoes (the dry, unmarinated type), cut into strips
1–1½ oz. (30–45 g) butter
1 clove garlic, chopped
salt, freshly ground black pepper, and thyme, to taste

Cook the pasta and sun-dried tomatoes in boiling water until the pasta is tender; drain. (The water may be reserved for soup, etc., since it will have some flavor from the tomatoes.)

Toss in the butter, garlic, salt, black pepper, and thyme.

VARIATION

Lumachine with Sun-dried Tomatoes and Yellow Squash: Tender, sweet summer squash adds a sunny note to this simple pasta: add 1 or 2 diced yellow summer squash — either yellow crookneck or golden zucchini (courgette) — to the cooking water with the pasta and sun-dried tomatoes. If yellow squash is not available, use zucchini. Mangetout (snow peas) or sugar snap peas are sweetly delicious cooked along with the squash and pasta.

SERVES 4

PREVIOUS PAGE ♦ *Broth-cooked Orzo with Lemon and Parsley (left), Fettuccine with a Confetti of Vegetables and Garlic–Mint Sauce (top), and Lumachine with Sun-dried Tomatoes (right)*
RIGHT ♦ *Wide Noodles with Garlic Butter, Fresh Sage, and Black Wrinkled Olives*

Wide Noodles with Garlic Butter, Fresh Sage, and Black Wrinkled Olives

Nuggets of salty black olives punctuate the delicacy of garlic-buttered wide noodles, while fresh sage adds its savor to this simple summer dish. Serve accompanied by sliced, sweet, ripe tomatoes, sprinkled with basil or marjoram, sea salt, and olive oil.

12 oz. (375 g) wide egg-pasta ribbons
1 oz. (30 g) unsalted butter, softened
1 tablespoon extra virgin olive oil
3–4 garlic cloves, chopped
1–2 tablespoons coarsely chopped fresh sage leaves
about 15 wrinkled black olives (oil- or salt-cured), pitted and halved

3 tablespoons freshly grated Parmesan cheese, or to taste
salt and freshly ground black pepper, to taste

Cook the pasta until *al dente*.

Meanwhile, mix the butter, olive oil, and garlic together.

Drain the pasta, then return to the pan and toss with the butter mixture, sage, and olives over a low to medium heat so that the pasta stays nice and hot and the butter melts evenly throughout the noodles.

Serve immediately, seasoned with salt and black pepper and sprinkled with Parmesan cheese.

SERVES 4

Orecchiette o Cavatieddi with Tomatoes and Arugula

From the deep south of Italy, this dish is usually prepared with older, strongly flavored specimens of arugula (rocket). For those who have only eaten arugula in salads, this dish is a revelation. And it couldn't be simpler or quicker to prepare; take care, though, that you cut the rocket into small enough lengths, as it can become stringy and hard to chew.
If you come across the delightfully twisted pasta shapes such as cavatieddi or gemelli, do try them with this lively sauce.

1 lb (500 g) orecchiette, cavatieddi, spaghetti or similar pasta shape
4–6 oz. (125–185 g) coarsely chopped arugula (rocket)
6–8 shallots or 3–4 garlic cloves, chopped
2 tablespoons extra virgin olive oil
1 lb (500 g) fresh or tinned tomatoes, chopped
salt and red chili pepper flakes or cayenne pepper, to taste

Cook the pasta until almost *al dente;* add the arugula, cook for a few moments longer, then drain.

Meanwhile, lightly sauté the shallots or garlic in the olive oil, then add the tomatoes. Cook over high heat until the sauce thickens, then season with salt and hot chili pepper flakes or cayenne pepper.

Toss the pasta and arugula with the tomato sauce and serve immediately.

VARIATIONS
Add arugula to the tomato sauce rather than the pasta. This works well when the arugula is on the older, spicier side.
Whole-wheat Pasta with Broccoli Tops: Prepare the recipe above, using whole-wheat (wholemeal) pasta instead of theorecchietteor cavatieddi, and broccoli tops (broccoli rabe) instead of the arugula (this needs rather more hot chili pepper flakes or cayenne pepper than the preceding recipe). Finish with a sprinkling of fresh herbs, such as basil and oregano, and freshly grated Parmesan, pecorino, or similar cheese.

SERVES 4–6

Fazzoletti di Seta (Handkerchiefs) of Pasta with Pesto

Delicate squares of homemade pasta, fazzoletti, are served tumbled artlessly into small piles on each plate to look like a dropped handkerchief. This simple dish is from the region of Liguria, where the basil scent of pesto wafts through every alleyway, shop, and window.
In Liguria the pasta is prepared from a dough made with white wine for added delicacy; I substitute shop-bought pasta squares, such as wonton noodles or other fresh pasta.
As with other simple dishes, all of the ingredients must be of the highest quality: tender, fresh-tasting pasta, homemade pesto (see p. 16), or a freshly made one from a delicatessen, and freshly grated pecorino, Romano, or Parmesan cheese.

12–16 oz. (375–500 g) flat, wide fresh pasta, such as wonton noodles or other pasta sheets, about 3 in. (7.5 cm) square
1½ oz. (45 g) butter
8 oz. (250 g) pesto (see p. 16)
freshly grated pecorino, Romano, or Parmesan cheese (about 2–3 tablespoons per person)

Boil the pasta until *al dente*; this will only take 2–3 minutes. Drain well and carefully, as delicate pasta tends to fall apart easily.

Toss the cooked pasta with the butter, then serve each portion immediately, topped with a generous helping of pesto and the grated cheese.

VARIATIONS
Pasta with Pesto and Mascarpone: Follow the recipe above, with the addition of a tablespoon or two of mascarpone on each portion of pasta. As you eat the pasta, the mascarpone dissolves into a creamy sauce that makes this delicious dish even better, and a worthy beginning to any special meal.
Pasta with Pesto and Goat Cheese: Spoon a small amount of a tangy fresh goat cheese onto each pesto-topped pasta portion.

SERVES 4–6

RIGHT ♦ *Orecchiette with Tomatoes and Arugula*

Whole-wheat Spaghetti with Goat Cheese, Fresh Tomatoes, and Olives

For this dish of exuberant and vivid flavors be sure to use whole-wheat (wholemeal) pasta imported from Italy (such as the de Cecco brand). It has a nutty flavor and supple texture, whereas other whole-wheat pasta cooks up to a slightly gummy consistency, with a taste that is heavy and almost sweet.

12–16 oz. (375–500 g) Italian whole-wheat
   (wholemeal) spaghetti
15 Italian or Greek black olives, pitted and coarsely
   chopped
15 green olives, pitted and coarsely chopped
3 garlic cloves, chopped
4 ripe tomatoes, peeled, seeded, and diced
1 cup (4 fl. oz., 100 ml) extra virgin olive oil,
   or more to taste
5 oz. (155 g) goat cheese, coarsely crumbled
1 oz. (30 g) fresh basil leaves, torn or coarsely cut up
freshly ground black pepper to taste

Cook the pasta until *al dente*.

Meanwhile, combine the black and green olives with the garlic, tomatoes, and olive oil.

Drain the pasta and toss with the olive mixture, then toss in the goat cheese, basil, and black pepper. Serve immediately.

SERVES 4

Fettuccine with Truffle Sauce

Because a dish takes under five minutes to prepare does not mean it is less than superb. Take this little concoction of buttered fettuccine tossed with chopped garlic and as much truffle as you can get your hands on. It is from the Italian province of Umbria; in Alba a similar dish is prepared using the heady white truffles instead of the black ones.

1 lb (500 g) fresh fettuccine
3 tablespoons extra virgin olive oil or 1½ oz. (45 g) butter
2 garlic cloves, finely chopped
1–2 oz. (30–60 g) black truffle paste
salt to taste

Cook the pasta until *al dente* (fresh fettuccine takes only a few minutes).

Drain and toss with the olive oil or butter and the garlic, then with the truffle paste. Season with salt and serve.

VARIATIONS

Fettuccine with Truffle Sauce and Strands of Multicolored Vegetables: Serve the pasta tossed with a selection of vegetables cut into matchsticks, then cooked in the water with the pasta: try 1 carrot, 1 celery stalk, 1 zucchini (courgette), and a handful of green beans.
Pasta with Truffle Cream: Toss in ⅓–½ cup (3–4 fl. oz., 90–125 ml) heavy (double) cream (or ¼ cup whipping cream or Italian mascarpone cream cheese), or to taste.
Gnocchi with Truffle Sauce: Substitute chewy potato gnocchi (available in many delicatessens and supermarkets) for the fettuccine. These little potato dumplings are particularly good with the savory truffle sauce.

SERVES 4–6

Rosemary-and-garlic-buttered Pasta

Rosemary-and-garlic butter is delicious melted onto any pasta, especially fresh pasta. Try it on wonton noodles, cheese-filled ravioli, or wide egg noodles, topped with a handful of coarsely grated Parmesan cheese.

12 oz. (375 g) pasta of choice
1–1½ oz. (30–45 g) butter, preferably unsalted, softened
2 garlic cloves, or to taste, finely chopped
2–4 tablespoons finely chopped fresh rosemary
salt and coarsely ground black pepper, to taste

Cook the pasta until *al dente*; drain.

Toss with the butter, garlic, and rosemary, and season with salt and black pepper. Serve at once.

SERVES 4

Buttered Bay-scented Capellini

Utterly simple with an elusive, subtle flavor. The bay leaves scent the thin strings of pasta, permeating each and every strand. While the quantity below makes enough to serve four, I often make enough for only one or two, as this is an awfully good late-night snack.

4–6 fresh or dried bay leaves
12 oz. (375 g) capellini
butter to taste
salt and freshly ground black pepper, to taste

Add the bay leaves to a large pot of salted water, then bring to the boil.

Add the capellini, cook until just tender, then drain. Remove the bay leaves.

Toss the hot drained pasta in plenty of butter, then add salt and black pepper to taste. Serve immediately.

SERVES 4

LEFT ♦ *Whole-wheat Spaghetti with Goat Cheese, Fresh Tomatoes, and Olives*

Pasta Aglio e Olio
(Pasta with Garlic and Olive Oil, Two Ways)

At its very simplest, Pasta Aglio e Olio is no more than al dente pasta tossed with chopped garlic and good olive oil. From here, the versions become numerous, with additions of fresh herbs and/or hot chili peppers, as well as the option of heating the garlic in the oil. If you use it raw it will be pungent, hot and strong, while if it is cooked it will be tastier and mellow.

While Pasta Aglio e Olio is not traditionally served with Parmesan cheese, I find that the occasional shake is delicious and adds even more variety.

3–6 garlic cloves, finely chopped, to taste
½ cup (4 fl. oz., 125 ml) extra virgin olive oil,
   or less if preferred
1 lb (500 g) spaghetti
salt and coarsely ground black pepper, to taste

Version 1: With Raw Garlic: Combine the garlic with the olive oil. Cook the pasta until *al dente*, then drain and toss with the garlic and oil. Season with salt and black pepper, and serve immediately.

Version 2: With Lightly Toasted Golden Garlic: Heat the garlic in the olive oil until golden. Remove from the heat and set aside. Cook the pasta until *al dente*, then drain and toss with the garlic and oil. Season with salt and black pepper and serve immediately.

VARIATIONS USING VERSION 2

With Hot Chili Pepper and Parsley: Add a generous pinch of hot red chili pepper flakes as you heat the garlic in the oil. Toss with the cooked pasta and a handful or two of chopped fresh parsley, preferably the flat-leafed Italian type.

With Cayenne Pepper, Parsley, and Lime: Prepare the basic recipe, adding parsley as above. Season forcefully with lots of cayenne pepper, and toss with the finely grated rind of 1 lime and the juice of 1–2 limes, or to taste. Also good with lemon.

With Capers: Add several teaspoons of capers to the hot chili pepper and parsley variation. A short squeeze or two of lemon juice is good, too.

With Basil Leaves: Add a small handful of torn or coarsely chopped fresh basil leaves to the oil as you heat the garlic.

With Cabbage, Italian Style: A favorite dish of mine, this is an excellent example of *cucina povera*, the cooking of the poor. In Italy one of the more unusual cabbage varieties, such as black cabbage, might be used, but I find that ordinary white or green cabbage works just fine.

Coarsely chop half a head or so of white or green cabbage and add to the pan along with the garlic and hot red chili pepper flakes (see first variation opposite). Sauté until tender and lightly browned, adding more oil, garlic, or chili pepper flakes if needed. Season with salt, then serve with pasta of choice.

SERVES 4–6

Whole-wheat Spaghetti with Toasted Garlic, Hot Chili Pepper, and Broccoli

Midnight-feast stuff, this, as long as you don't have to be anywhere polite the next morning.

12–16 oz. (375–500 g) whole-wheat (wholemeal)
   spaghetti
1 large bunch broccoli, cut into small florets
8–10 garlic cloves, coarsely chopped
4 tablespoons extra virgin olive oil
1 dried hot red chili pepper, broken into several
   pieces
salt and freshly ground black pepper, to taste

Cook the spaghetti until half-done; add the broccoli and continue cooking until pasta and broccoli are *al dente*.

Meanwhile, heat the garlic in the olive oil with the chili pepper. When the garlic is golden, remove the pan from the heat and remove the bits of chili pepper. Discard the chili pepper and set the oil aside.

Drain the pasta and broccoli and toss with the reserved garlic and olive oil mixture. Season with salt and black pepper to taste.

SERVES 4–6

RIGHT ♦ *Whole-wheat Spaghetti with Toasted Garlic, Hot Chili Pepper, and Broccoli*

Buckwheat Soba with Peas and Cream

Japanese flat buckwheat pasta, also known as soba, tastes of the grain it is ground from: earthy, whole-wheat (wholemeal), and almost sweet. It is traditionally served with clear soup in Japan and Korea, and is also popular served cold, sometimes with a poached egg, and with spicy condiments such as chili oil, wasabi (strong horseradish) paste, scallions (spring onions), and even chips of ice for a refreshing summer snack.

The following recipe, however, uses the soba in a distinctly Western way: tossed with peas, cream, and Parmesan cheese. It is a rich and Alfredo-like mixture, but unusual for its buckwheat flavor.

8 oz. (250 g) buckwheat soba, preferably the flat, fettuccine-like noodles
2 oz. (60 g) butter
2 garlic cloves, chopped
6–8 oz. (185–250 g) fresh and blanched, or frozen, peas
1 cup (8 fl. oz., 250 ml) light (single) cream
4 oz. (125 g) Parmesan cheese, freshly grated
freshly ground black pepper, to taste

Cook the buckwheat soba in boiling water until *al dente*; drain.

Melt the butter with the garlic, then add the peas and cook until the peas are cooked through if fresh, or heated through if frozen. Pour in the cream and heat until bubbles form around the edge of the pan.

Toss with the hot, drained pasta and Parmesan cheese, then serve immediately seasoned with black pepper (it will most likely not need salt as the Parmesan cheese is salty).

SERVES 4

Lockshen and Cheese

Lockshen is the Yiddish word for noodles, and this is the dish I grew up eating — the dish I end up cooking whenever I am in the mood for a little comfort, pasta-style.

Cottage cheese is eaten with pasta in a variety of ways throughout Europe. In Eastern Europe, interestingly, the dish might be sweet, with sugar and cinnamon replacing the salt and pepper. In Italy, it is fresh ricotta, cottage cheese's Mediterranean cousin, that pairs with pasta for this comforting and wholesome dish.

I like lockshen with garlic, and lots of it (see Variation below).

12 oz. (375 g) pasta of choice, preferably short, chubby shapes or curly twists
1½ oz. (45 g) butter, or to taste
12 oz. (375 g) plain cottage cheese
salt and freshly ground black pepper, to taste

Cook the pasta until *al dente*; drain.

Mix in the butter well, then serve each portion topped with a dollop of cottage cheese and sprinkled with salt and pepper. Alternatively, you can toss it all together, then serve.

VARIATION

Marlena's Cottage Cheese and Pasta: My favorite deviation from the above involves tossing the pasta with olive oil rather than butter, and sprinkling the cottage cheese with a generous amount of raw, chopped garlic, before serving. Sometimes I add a sprinkling of fresh herbs, such as basil, oregano, etc. This dish invigorates as it comforts, and my two daughters have become addicted to it, as has our cat.

SERVES 4

LEFT ♦ *Buckwheat Soba with Peas and Cream*

Whole-wheat Spaghetti with Tomatoes, Green Beans, Pesto, and Goat Cheese

Chewy and nutty-tasting whole-wheat (wholemeal) spaghetti partners exuberantly with garlicky tomatoes, green beans, pesto, and goat cheese. This makes a complex dish, far more flavorful than its simple preparation would indicate.

- 3 garlic cloves, finely chopped
- 3 tablespoons extra virgin olive oil
- 2 fresh or drained tinned tomatoes, diced, and seeded
- 1 lb (500 g) whole-wheat (wholemeal) spaghetti, preferably an Italian brand
- 4 oz. (125 g) green beans, cut into bite-sized lengths
- 3 heaped tablespoons pesto, or to taste
- 2–3 oz. (60–90 g) goat cheese, preferably a fresh, light garlic- or chive-flavored one, crumbled

Heat the garlic in the olive oil just until it smells wonderful but is not yet turning golden. Add the tomatoes and cook for a minute or two, then remove from the heat.

Meanwhile, cook the spaghetti until half-done, then add the green beans and continue to cook until the beans are crisp-tender and bright green and the pasta is *al dente*.

Drain and toss in the garlicky-tomato mixture. Serve immediately, each portion topped with pesto and goat cheese.

VARIATIONS

Whole-wheat Spaghetti with Green Beans, Black Olive Paste, and Goat Cheese: Spoon black olive paste on to each portion instead of pesto, together with a sprinkling of chopped fresh basil or parsley, and a dollop of goat cheese.

Whole-wheat Spaghetti with Green Beans and Pesto: Drain and toss with several large tablespoons of Pesto Genovese (see p. 16). Serve sprinkled with Parmesan cheese or pecorino Sardo.

SERVES 4–6

Spaghetti al Zenzero
(Spaghetti with Garlic, Ginger, Hot Chili Pepper, Mint, and Basil)

An unusual variation on the ubiquitous Roman dish of pasta with olive oil and garlic. The fresh ginger and hot chili pepper give a spicy kick, while the mint and basil are leafy, sweet, and fresh.

12–16 oz. (375–500 g) spaghetti
6–10 garlic cloves, coarsely chopped
2-in. (5-cm) piece of fresh ginger root, unpeeled, cut into 4–5 thin slices
pinch of red chili pepper flakes
⅓ cup (3 fl. oz., 75 ml) extra virgin olive oil
salt to taste
2 tablespoons thinly sliced or coarsely chopped fresh basil leaves
2 tablespoons thinly sliced or coarsely chopped fresh mint leaves

Cook the spaghetti until *al dente.*

Meanwhile, heat the garlic, ginger, and red chili pepper flakes in the olive oil, cooking until the garlic becomes golden around the edges; do not brown. Remove and discard the ginger slices.

Drain the spaghetti, then toss with the flavored oil. Add salt to taste.

Serve immediately, tossed with the basil and mint.

VARIATION
For Roman-style spaghetti with garlic, mint, and a whiff of lemon, follow the above recipe but omit the ginger and basil. Increase the amount of red chili pepper to taste, and serve the pasta either hot or at room temperature, with lemon wedges or a dash of balsamic vinegar.

SERVES 4

LEFT ♦ *Whole-wheat Spaghetti with Tomatoes, Green Beans, Pesto, and Goat Cheese*

Spaghetti or Penne with Sun-dried Tomatoes and Goat Cheese

12–16 oz. (375–500 g) spaghetti or penne
20 sun-dried tomatoes, either dry or marinated in oil, cut into strips
3–4 garlic cloves, chopped
3 tablespoons extra virgin olive oil, or to taste
salt, freshly ground black pepper, and thyme, or crumbled dried mixed herbs, to taste
5 oz. (155 g) fresh, tangy goat cheese, coarsely crumbled

Cook the pasta in boiling water until *al dente.* (If using dry sun-dried tomatoes, cook them with the pasta; if using marinated, add to the cooked pasta with the other ingredients.)

Drain the pasta and toss with the garlic, olive oil, salt, black pepper, herbs, and sun-dried tomatoes (if using marinated ones).

Toss with the goat cheese and serve immediately.

SERVES 4–6

Tarragon and Lemon Pasta with Sharp Cheese

Admittedly it sounds unlikely, but the combination is delicious, all the more so for its unexpected flavors. The tarragon and lemon lighten up the cloak of melting cheese.

12 oz. (375 g) short pasta of choice
1½ oz. (45 g) unsalted butter
juice of ½ lemon, or to taste
½ teaspoon dried tarragon, or to taste, crumbled between the fingers
6–8 oz. (185–250 g) sharp (aged) Cheddar, or mature Cheddar cheese, coarsely grated
salt and freshly ground black pepper, to taste

Cook the pasta until *al dente;* drain.

Toss with the butter, lemon juice, tarragon, cheese, salt, if needed, and black pepper. Serve immediately.

SERVES 4

Tiny Elbow Pasta With Basil, Parsley, and Lime

The sweetness of basil pairs with the fresh parsley and the jolt of sour lime in this invigorating, simple dish. The very tiny elbow pasta is my favorite here — especially the brand Federici which is marked simply 'quick-cooking macaroni'. Do not be misled into thinking that this is an inauthentic product. It is the tiniest, sweetest, most succulent elbow macaroni you can imagine. And, yes, it is quick cooking — about 2 to 3 minutes.

4 garlic cloves, coarsely chopped
3–4 tablespoons extra virgin olive oil
15–20 basil leaves, torn up coarsely
12 oz. (375 g) small elbow-shaped macaroni
handful of parsley, coarsely chopped
grated rind and juice of ½–1 lime, to taste
salt and freshly ground black pepper or cayenne
   pepper, to taste

Heat the garlic in the olive oil until golden; remove from the heat and add the basil. The basil should wilt in the hot oil and go bright green and glossy.

Cook the pasta until *al dente*, then drain.

Toss the pasta in the basil and garlic oil, together with the parsley and grated lime rind and juice. Season with salt and black or cayenne pepper, and serve immediately.

SERVES 4

Pasta with Black Olive and Rosemary Cream

This silken sauce is simple: a purée of inky black olives and a whiff of rosemary, with rich cream. A sprinkling of Parmesan cheese pulls it all together.

12 oz. (375 g) fettuccine
3 tablespoons black olive paste
2 teaspoons chopped fresh rosemary, or to taste
1 cup (8 fl. oz., 250 ml) light (single) cream
1 oz. (30 g) butter, preferably unsalted
salt and freshly ground black pepper, to taste
freshly grated Parmesan cheese, to taste

Cook the pasta until *al dente*.

Meanwhile, combine the olive paste and rosemary, then stir in the cream; set aside.

Drain the pasta and toss first with the butter, then with the sauce. Season with salt and black pepper, and add Parmesan cheese to taste.

VARIATION

With Goat Cheese or Feta Cheese: Instead of Parmesan, toss the dressed pasta with mild, creamy goat cheese or tangy feta cheese, crumbled, and let it melt in. Include a clove of chopped garlic in the olive paste mixture.

SERVES 4

Spaghetti with Double Tomato Relish and Fresh Mozzarella

This fresh, salady mixture of sun-dried tomatoes, fresh tomatoes, masses of basil, and garlic, all bound up in olive oil, makes a delicious sauce for hot pasta, especially with diced mozzarella cheese melting creamily in.

1 lb (500 g) spaghetti
6–8 very fresh tomatoes, diced (and peeled,
   if you prefer)
15 oil-marinated sun-dried tomatoes, coarsely
   chopped (or 5–6 tablespoons sun-dried tomato
   paste (purée))
several large handfuls fresh basil, thinly sliced or
   coarsely chopped
3 garlic cloves, chopped
3–4 tablespoons extra virgin olive oil
salt and freshly ground black pepper, to taste
8–12 oz. (250–375 g) fresh mozzarella (the light,
   white, milky cheese that comes in a watery brine,
   not the drier, firmer, pizza-topping), diced

Cook the spaghetti until *al dente*.

Meanwhile, mix the fresh and sun-dried tomatoes with the basil, garlic, and olive oil. Taste for seasoning, adding salt and black pepper, and more garlic, if needed.

Drain the spaghetti; toss with the sauce and mozzarella cheese and serve immediately.

SERVES 4–6

Spaghetti with Green Beans, Goat Cheese, Garlic, and Basil

1 lb (500 g) spaghetti
12 oz. (375 g) green beans, cut into bite-sized
    lengths
5 garlic cloves, chopped
3 tablespoons extra virgin olive oil
4 oz. (125 g) goat cheese, crumbled
salt and freshly ground black pepper, to taste
handful of fresh basil leaves, torn or cut up

Cook the spaghetti until half-done, then add the green beans and continue cooking until both are *al dente*.

Meanwhile, combine the garlic and olive oil.

Drain the pasta, toss with the garlic and olive oil, then with the goat cheese. Season with salt and black pepper, add the basil, then serve.

VARIATIONS

Pasta with Fava Beans and Goat Cheese: This combination is very popular in many parts of Italy, such as the islands, where goat cheese is more common than cows' milk cheese, as it is easier to raise goats than cows in these mountainous regions.

Follow the recipe above but use peeled fava beans instead of green beans. If they are very young you do not need to peel their skin after you remove them from the pod, but shops seldom sell such tender young beans, so use your own judgement.

Pasta with Fava Beans, Goat Cheese, and Black Olives: Add a handful of diced, oil-cured black olives to the above recipe.

SERVES 4–6

BELOW ♦ *Spaghetti with Green Beans, Goat Cheese, Garlic, and Basil*

Garlicky Pasta with Fresh Green Herbs

This is an excellent dish to throw together in spring and summer when herbs are abundant. Cheese would only interfere with the herby flavors, but be sure to add enough salt and pepper. The flavor and character depends on the choice and quantity of herbs used. Use larger amounts of milder herbs, such as parsley, and smaller amounts of pungent ones, such as fresh oregano or sage.

1 lb (500 g) spaghetti
8 garlic cloves, coarsely chopped
¼–⅓ cup (2–3 fl. oz., 60–90 ml) extra virgin
    olive oil
selection of chopped fresh herbs: 1 oz. (30 g) fresh
    parsley and/or basil; several tablespoons each
    chives, marjoram, thyme, sage, oregano,
    rosemary, tarragon, etc.
salt and freshly ground black pepper, to taste

Cook spaghetti until *al dente.*

Meanwhile, heat the garlic in the olive oil until it smells fragrant (just a few moments). Toss the herbs in the garlicky hot oil; remove from the heat.

Drain the pasta. Toss in the pan with the garlicky oil and herbs. Season generously with salt and black pepper.

SERVES 4–6

Leslie Forbes' Last-minute Spicy Pasta with Red Pesto and Asparagus

Leslie cooks the sort of strongly flavored, simple yet imaginative food that I adore. She is always adding this and that ingredient that one might think would clash, yet they combine harmoniously, like so much gastronomical jazz improvisation. Such is the case with this pasta recipe, thrown together with what was on hand in the Forbes kitchen.

1 lb (500 g) penne
8 oz. (250 g) asparagus, tough ends broken off,
    the stalks cut into bite-sized pieces
2–3 tablespoons chilied olive oil (see p. 17)
6½-oz. (200-g) jar red pesto, or use homemade
    pesto (see p. 16)
2 oz. (60 g) Parmesan cheese, shaved

Boil the pasta until about half-cooked, then add the asparagus and continue cooking until the pasta is *al dente* and the asparagus is crisp-tender; drain.

Toss with the chilied olive oil, then the red pesto, and serve immediately, topped with the Parmesan cheese.

SERVES 4–6

Pasta with Creamy Pesto and Blue Cheese Sauce

This rich dish is perfumed with basil and garlic, and the pungent flavor of blue cheese is smoothed over with cream. It has the flavors of Torta Basilica, that northern Italian concoction of Gorgonzola, basil, and mascarpone cheese. A handful of toasted pine nuts gives the dish a crunchy texture, but if unavailable, simply omit, as it will be delicious regardless. And it is equally good hot or cold.

12 oz. (375 g) fresh pasta, delicate dried fettuccine,
    or the sturdier penne
8 oz. (250 g) blue cheese, crumbled
⅓ cup (3 fl. oz., 90 ml) single (light) cream
3 tablespoons pesto (see p. 16)
2 garlic cloves, finely chopped
3 tablespoons pine nuts
salt and freshly ground black pepper, to taste
thinly sliced fresh basil leaves (optional)

Cook the pasta until *al dente.*

Meanwhile, mix together the blue cheese, cream, pesto, and garlic.

Toast the pine nuts in an ungreased, heavy skillet (frying pan) until lightly browned.

Drain the pasta and toss with the sauce; season with salt, if needed, and black pepper. Serve immediately, sprinkled with the toasted pine nuts, and the fresh basil, if using.

SERVES 4

LEFT ♦ *Leslie Forbes' Last-minute Spicy Pasta with Red Pesto and Asparagus (top), and Garlicky Pasta with Fresh Green Herbs (bottom)*

Spaghetti with Garlic Butter and Walnuts

Golden sautéed garlic is combined with warm, toasted nuts, then tossed with spaghetti, Parmesan cheese, and a small amount of mascarpone or cream, to gild this already rich dish.

12 oz. (375 g) spaghetti
4–6 garlic cloves, coarsely chopped
2 oz. (60 g) butter
4 oz. (125 g) shelled walnuts, halved and coarsely chopped
½ cup (4 fl. oz., 125 ml) mascarpone cheese or whipping (double) cream
1½ oz. (45 g) Parmesan cheese, freshly grated
salt and freshly ground black pepper, to taste

Cook the spaghetti until *al dente*.

Meanwhile, sauté the garlic in the butter until fragrant and lightly golden, then add the walnuts and swirl around in the garlic butter. Remove from the heat and stir in the mascarpone or cream. Set aside.

Drain the spaghetti; toss with the sauce, then with the Parmesan cheese. Season with salt and black pepper and serve immediately.

VARIATION

Ravioli con Salsa de Noci: For this Ligurian classic, use spinach-and-cheese-stuffed ravioli instead of spaghetti, and do not fry the garlic and walnuts. Rather, increase the amount of walnuts to 7 oz. (225 g), then grind them in a grinder or food processor until finely chopped. Combine the ground nuts with the garlic, butter, mascarpone or cream, and Parmesan cheese and mix well. Toss with the cooked ravioli and serve immediately, sprinkled with a handful of finely chopped fresh basil.

SERVES 4–6

Fettuccine with Mascarpone, Pine Nuts, and Basil

This is very rich, with fresh, fragrant basil to lighten and enliven it. The mixture of basil and cheese should coat the pasta rather than drown it. Lightly toasted pine nuts add texture to this plateful of classic flavors.
Serve as a first course, followed by something savory and strongly flavored.

2 oz. (60 g) pine nuts
12–16 oz. (375–500 g) fresh fettuccine, the most delicate you can find
1 oz. (30 g) butter, preferably unsalted, softened
several large tablespoons mascarpone cheese, softened and at room temperature
salt and freshly ground black pepper, to taste

4 tablespoons freshly grated Parmesan cheese, plus extra to serve
handful of fresh basil leaves, torn or coarsely chopped

Toast the pine nuts in an ungreased heavy skillet (frying pan) over medium heat until flecked lightly brown, tossing them as they turn for even browning. Set aside.

Cook the pasta until *al dente*. Drain and toss first with the butter, then with the mascarpone cheese, then with the toasted pine nuts, salt and black pepper, and Parmesan cheese. Sprinkle with the basil and serve immediately, offering extra Parmesan cheese separately.

SERVES 4–6

LEFT ♦ *Spaghetti with Garlic Butter and Walnuts*
BELOW ♦ *Fettuccine with Mascarpone, Pine Nuts, and Basil*

Farfalle Verde with Broccoli and Red Sweet Pepper in Spicy Tomato Sauce

4–6 garlic cloves, chopped
½–1 red sweet pepper (capsicum), thinly sliced
  or coarsely chopped
2 tablespoons extra virgin olive oil
1 bunch broccoli, cut into florets, stems peeled and
  diced
handful of fresh and blanched, or frozen, peas
8 oz. (250 g) fresh or tinned tomatoes, chopped
¼ teaspoon cayenne pepper, or to taste
generous pinch of thyme
10–12 oz. (310–375 g) farfalle verde, or other
  green pasta
salt to taste
grated Parmesan, pecorino or Romano cheese
  (optional)

Lightly sauté the garlic and red sweet pepper in the olive oil; add the broccoli and a few tablespoons of water. Cover and cook over high heat for a minute or two until just tender. Add the peas and tomatoes, season with cayenne pepper and thyme, cover, and cook for another 5–10 minutes.

Meanwhile, cook the pasta until *al dente;* drain and toss with the sauce. Season with salt, if needed, and serve with grated cheese if desired.

SERVES 4

Fettuccine with Green Olives, Goat Cheese, and Thyme

Goat cheese and green olives make a tangy yet lightly creamy sauce for pasta.

12–16 oz. (375–500 g) fettuccine or pasta of choice
2–3 garlic cloves, chopped
3–4 tablespoons chopped green olives or green
  olive paste
½ teaspoon fresh thyme or ¼ teaspoon dried thyme
3 tablespoons extra virgin olive oil
5 oz. (155 g) goat cheese, crumbled
red chili pepper flakes, or coarsely ground black
  pepper, to taste

Cook the pasta until *al dente.*

Meanwhile, warm the garlic, olives, and thyme gently in the olive oil; do not brown.

Drain the pasta and toss with the garlic and olive mixture and the goat cheese, warming it over a low heat so that the cheese melts into a clinging, creamy sauce.

Season with red chili pepper flakes or black pepper and serve immediately.

SERVES 4

Broccoli Carbonara (Pasta and Broccoli Tossed with Beaten Egg and Cheese)

Adding a small amount of butter at the end gives the pasta a certain glossiness and richness. As always, when you are preparing a dish in which eggs are only lightly cooked, seek out a reliable source of free-range, salmonella-free specimens.

12 oz. (375 g) lumachine (small shells) or elbow
  shapes
10–12 oz. (310–375 g) broccoli, cut into bite-sized
  florets, the stems peeled and sliced
1 egg, lightly beaten
2 tablespoons milk
3 oz. (90 g) Parmesan cheese, freshly grated
salt and freshly ground black pepper, to taste
½–1 oz. (15–30 g) unsalted butter (at room
  temperature)

Cook the pasta in boiling water until half-done (about 4 minutes). Add the broccoli and continue cooking until the pasta is *al dente* and the broccoli bright green and just cooked; drain.

Mix the egg with the milk and half the cheese, then toss the hot, drained pasta and broccoli with this mixture, letting the heat cook the egg as it tosses. Add the remaining Parmesan cheese, salt if needed, black pepper, and the butter, tossing to mix well. Serve immediately.

SERVES 4

RIGHT ◆ *Fusilli Verde with Broccoli and Red Sweet Pepper in Spicy Tomato Sauce*

Pasta with Sauces of Vegetables, Cheeses, and Beans

Pastas of all sizes and shapes combine deliciously with nearly any and every vegetable, cheese or bean imaginable. As the year unfolds, so will the pasta on your table change: mushrooms, zucchini (courgettes), juicy tomatoes, crisp green beans, fresh aromatic herbs, aubergine (eggplant), colorful peppers, tender young peas or sweet carrots. Cheeses, especially strongly flavored ones, are natural partners for pasta. There are few dishes more comforting than a plate of pasta tossed with a generous amount of cheese, hot and melting into the bowlful.

◆ ◆ ◆

High-protein beans combined with chewy, supple pasta also make satisfying dishes.
The range is wide: white kidney (cannellini) beans, tender pale green flageolets, black-eyed peas, mealy butter
beans or lima beans, red kidney beans and nutty chickpeas (garbanzos), plus lentils of all colors. You can
substitute tinned beans for dried beans in most recipes, but adjust the salt; most tinned beans are overly saline.
Soy products fill out pasta sauces, too, adding body and protein. For recipes using tofu, see Far Eastern Pasta
(pp. 136–151). Soups and Stews (pp. 20–35) includes other pasta dishes with beans.

♦ ♦ ♦

Gingered Fusilli Lunghi with Corn, Zucchini, and Sweet Peppers

This sauce is a lively mélange of sautéed onions, garlic, and hot and sweet peppers (capsicums), smoothed out with a glistening of Greek-style yogurt or sour cream. The thick winding twists of fusilli lunghi are very nice in this sauce, but rotelle (wagon wheels), cavatappi (hollow corkscrews) or any chunky pasta would be good, too.

2 onions, chopped
3 garlic cloves, chopped
1 green sweet pepper (capsicum), chopped
2 tablespoons extra virgin olive oil
½–1 fresh red chili pepper, seeded and chopped
2 small zucchini (courgettes), diced
1–1½ cups (8–12 fl. oz., 250–375 ml) vegetable broth (see p. 15)
kernels from 2–3 ears of corn
8 oz. (250 g) diced fresh or tinned tomatoes
¼ teaspoon grated fresh ginger root, or to taste
3–4 tablespoons Greek-style yogurt, crème frâiche, or sour cream
12 oz. (375 g) fusilli lunghi, or other pasta of choice
4 oz. (125 g) melting white cheese such as mozzarella, milk Cheddar, etc., diced
3–4 tablespoons chopped fresh coriander leaves

Lightly sauté the onions, garlic, and green sweet pepper in olive oil until they have just softened, then add the chili pepper and zucchini. Cook for 5 minutes, or until the zucchini has also softened, then add the broth and increase the heat, letting the broth evaporate to about half its original volume.

Add the corn and tomatoes. Cook over a high heat for 5–10 minutes, or until the corn is cooked through and the mixture has thickened and is sauce-like, but remains thinner than most pasta sauces.

Season with ginger root and stir in the yogurt or crème frâiche or sour cream. Keep the sauce warm.

Cook the pasta until *al dente*, then drain. Toss the pasta with the sauce and cheese. Sprinkle with the coriander leaves and serve.

SERVES 4–6

Spaghetti with Green Beans, Tomato, and Olives

4–5 garlic cloves, coarsely chopped
¼ cup (2 fl. oz., 60 ml) extra virgin olive oil
handful of fresh basil leaves, coarsely torn
8 oz. (250 g) green or string beans, as tender and fresh as possible
10–15 ripe tomatoes, diced
pinch of sugar
salt and freshly ground black pepper, to taste
1 lb. (500 g) spaghetti
10 oil-cured black olives, pitted and diced
freshly grated Parmesan cheese or other grating cheese, to serve

Heat the garlic in the olive oil until fragrant and lightly golden, then add the basil and the beans. Cook for a few moments, then add the tomatoes. Cook over a medium heat, adding a little water if necessary, until the mixture is sauce-like. Season with the sugar and salt and pepper.

Cook the pasta until *al dente*, then drain. Toss the pasta with the sauce, sprinkle with the black olives, and serve. Offer Parmesan cheese separately.

VARIATION
If yellow wax beans are available, add a handful along with the green beans.

SERVES 4–6

PREVIOUS PAGE ♦ *Spaghetti with Green Beans, Tomato, and Olives (left), and Gingered Fusilli Lunghi with Corn, Zucchini, and Sweet Peppers (right)*

RIGHT ♦ *Penne alla Puttanesca (Pasta with Olives, Capers, and Tomatoes)*

Penne alla Puttanesca (Pasta with Olives, Capers, and Tomatoes)

The lusty sauces made with garlic, tomatoes, olives and capers are often known as 'whore's style'. Don't serve cheese with this dish: just a last-minute sprinkling of parsley, and perhaps a little extra hot pepper.

4 tablespoons extra virgin olive oil
4–6 garlic cloves, chopped
2 pickled peperoncini (Italian or Greek bottled spicy peppers), chopped
2 lbs. (1 kg) ripe tomatoes, peeled, diced, and drained of excess juice, or 1 ½ tins (14 oz., 435 g tins) of chopped tomatoes
2 tablespoons tomato paste (purée)
pinch of sugar (optional)
about 20 kalamata olives, pitted and quartered
1–2 tablespoons capers
salt, to taste
1 lb. (500 g) penne
2 tablespoons chopped fresh parsley and/or fresh basil

Heat the olive oil, garlic, and peperoncini together until the garlic is fragrant and beginning to color.

Add the tomatoes, tomato paste, and the sugar (if needed), and bring the mixture to the boil. Reduce the heat and simmer for 15 minutes. Remove from the heat, add the olives, capers, and salt (if needed). Set aside, but keep warm.

Meanwhile, cook the pasta until *al dente*, then drain. Toss with the sauce, then serve sprinkled with the parsley and/or basil.

SERVES 4–6

Lemon-scented Couscous with Artichokes, Olives, and Sun-dried Tomatoes

Couscous is a tiny grain-like pasta made of hard semolina wheat, traditionally favored throughout North Africa as well as in Sicily. In recent years it has made its way into French cuisine as well as Californian and British.
The little pellets of pasta are usually sold pre-steamed so that they only need to be steeped in a hot savory sauce to plump them up into a luscious grain dish. In Morocco, Tunisia, and Sicily, couscous is usually steamed over a spicy stew filled with vegetables, meat, or fish. For my favorite vegetarian version, refer to my book, Hot & Spicy *(Grafton Books).*
Here we have a different sort of couscous; more Mediterranean and contemporary in flavor. It is cooked in the lemon-scented broth, then topped with a mixture of artichokes, sun-dried tomatoes, and olives.

2 large heads garlic, cloves separated and peeled
2 tablespoons extra virgin olive oil
6 artichokes (prepared as on p. 18), blanched and sliced
1 cup (8 fl. oz., 250 ml) dry white wine
¼ teaspoon dried thyme or herbes de Provence
2½ cups (1 imp. pint, 625 ml) vegetable broth (see p. 15), plus extra as needed
2 lemons, cut into quarters
15–20 black Italian- or Greek-style olives
5–10 oil-marinated sun-dried tomatoes, quartered or sliced into strips
12 oz. (375 g) instant couscous
1½ oz. (45 g) butter

Place the garlic cloves in a baking dish and toss with the olive oil. Bake in the oven at 375°F (190°C) for about 10 minutes, or until the garlic begins to brown lightly.

Add the blanched and sliced artichoke hearts, white wine, herbs, half the vegetable broth, and half the lemon quarters. Bake for another 20–30 minutes, until the liquid is reduced in volume to 16 fl. oz. (500 ml) and the artichokes are lightly browned.

Remove the dish from the oven and take out the cooked lemon quarters. Add the olives and sun-dried tomatoes, plus the remaining broth, and return the dish to the oven to heat through. Remove from the oven and pour about half the liquid into a saucepan. Return the

artichoke mixture to the oven to stay warm and continue roasting while you make the couscous (10–15 minutes).

Add enough extra broth to the pan to make it up to 2½ cups (1 imp. pint, 625 ml). Heat until almost boiling; squeeze remaining lemon quarters into the pan. Pour this over the couscous, dot with the butter, cover and leave to absorb the sauce and plump up (about 10 minutes).

Serve the hot couscous topped with the artichoke, olive, and sun-dried tomato mixture, plus the sauce it has cooked in.

SERVES 4–6

Spaghetti with Orange-scented Tomato Sauce

A squeeze of orange juice in a simple sauce of garlic- and basil-seasoned tomatoes adds an unusual and delightfully subtle nuance.

3 tablespoons extra virgin olive oil
2–3 garlic cloves, coarsely chopped
10–15 fresh basil leaves
2 lbs. (1 kg) ripe tomatoes, diced, or 1½ tins (14 oz., 435 g tins) chopped tomatoes
salt, to taste
juice of 1 orange
small shake of Tabasco sauce
1 lb. (500 g) spaghetti

Heat 2 tablespoons of the olive oil with the garlic and half the basil leaves. When the garlic colors, add the tomatoes and salt. Cook over high heat for 15–20 minutes, until the sauce has thickened.

Add the orange juice, season with the Tabasco sauce, and continue to cook over high heat for about 5 more minutes. Adjust the seasoning if necessary.

Cook the spaghetti until *al dente*, then drain.

Toss the hot drained spaghetti with the sauce. Drizzle the last tablespoon of olive oil over, sprinkle with the remaining basil leaves, and serve.

SERVES 4–6

RIGHT ♦ *Lemon-scented Couscous with Artichokes, Olives, and Sun-dried Tomatoes*

Pasta with Red, Yellow and Green Sweet Peppers, and Black Olives

Slow-baked sweet peppers (capsicums), mixed with slaty black olives and a splash of tomato and tossed with thin spaghettini or capellini, are delicious. Add a dash of balsamic vinegar at the end for a tangy accent and to help round out the flavor.

3 green sweet peppers (capsicums), diced
2 yellow sweet peppers (capsicums), diced
2 red sweet peppers (capsicums), diced
15 garlic cloves, chopped
salt and freshly ground black pepper, to taste
3–4 tablespoons extra virgin olive oil
4–6 ripe tomatoes, diced, or 4–6 oz. (125–185 g)
    diced tinned tomatoes
10–15 black olives (kalamata or oil-cured),
    pitted and halved
finely chopped fresh thyme, marjoram, basil, or
    other herb, to serve
dash of balsamic vinegar
1 lb. (500 g) pasta of choice: either long strands
    such as fettuccine or chunky shapes such as
    seashells, penne, etc.
coarsely grated or shaved Parmesan cheese, to serve

Place the sweet peppers and garlic in a flat earthenware dish, then toss with the salt, pepper, and olive oil. Bake in the oven, uncovered, at 400°F (200°C) for 1½ hours, tossing once or twice during this time. Add the tomatoes and return to the oven for another 30 minutes.

Remove from the oven and add the olives and herbs. Season with a dash of balsamic vinegar, and keep warm.

Cook the pasta until *al dente,* then drain. Toss with the sweet pepper mixture, adding more herbs if you like. Serve sprinkled with the Parmesan cheese.

VARIATION
Serve the above pasta sprinkled with goat cheese instead of Parmesan cheese, and let it melt in seductively.
Piperade Pasta: Cook 1 lb. (500 g) of spaghetti until *al dente;* drain. Toss with 2 lightly beaten eggs mixed with a generous amount of freshly grated Parmesan cheese. Combine with the vegetable mixture, omitting the olives. Sprinkle with several tablespoons of chopped fresh basil.

SERVES 6

Penne or Conchiglie Tricolore with Garlic and Tomato Sauce

These multi-hued pasta shapes are lovely with a sauce made from a good simple sauté of garlic and tomatoes. It's a lusty, straightforward sauce that is good with plain pasta as well.

1 lb. (500 g) multicolored penne or seashell pasta
6–8 garlic cloves, coarsely chopped
3 tablespoons extra virgin olive oil
2 lbs. (1 kg) ripe tomatoes, diced, or 1½ tins
    (14 oz., 435 g tins) tomatoes, well drained
salt and freshly ground black pepper, to taste
pinch of sugar
3–6 large fresh basil leaves, very thinly sliced
freshly grated Parmesan cheese, to serve (optional)

Cook the pasta until *al dente.* Warm the garlic in the olive oil until it is fragrant and just beginning to color. Add the tomatoes. Cook over medium to high heat for 5–8 minutes. Season with the salt, pepper and sugar and set aside for a moment or two.

Drain the pasta and toss it with the tomato sauce. Serve sprinkled with the basil and with Parmesan cheese (if using).

VARIATION
Ditalini, Spaghetti, Green Beans, and Peas with Garlic and Tomato Sauce: The combination of tiny circles of ditalini and long strands of spaghetti, slashes of green bean and small dots of peas is whimsical and visually delightful. Vary the proportions of vegetables and pasta to taste.

Prepare the tomato sauce as above. Begin to cook about 6 oz. (185 g) ditalini. After 3–4 minutes, when it is almost *al dente,* add a large handful of fresh green beans cut into bite-sized lengths, and about 6 oz. (185 g) of spaghetti. Continue cooking for another few minutes, then add about 4 oz. (125 g) of fresh or frozen peas. Cook for a minute or two more, until all the pasta is *al dente,* then drain and serve with the garlic and tomato sauce.

SERVES 4–6

RIGHT ♦ *Pasta with Red, Yellow and Green Sweet Peppers, and Black Olives*

Macaroni with Roasted Green Sweet Peppers, Tomatoes, and Goat Cheese

Strongly flavored with the taste of Italy's sun-drenched South, this dish tastes fresh and vibrant. That fresh quality, however, depends upon ripe, sweet, tangy tomatoes: if tomatoes like these are not available, another recipe is probably your best bet.

2 green sweet peppers (capsicums)
4 garlic cloves, chopped
3–4 tablespoons extra virgin olive oil
8–10 small, very ripe tomatoes, cut into eighths
12 oz. (375 g) short macaroni
1 tablespoon tomato paste (purée)
5 oz. (155 g) fresh goat cheese, preferably
   garlic- and herb-flavored
dried oregano, crumbled, to taste

salt and freshly ground black pepper, to taste
freshly grated cheese such as Parmesan or other
   hard grating cheese, to serve

Roast the green sweet peppers (see p. 19), then cut them into large dice.

Heat half the garlic in about 2 tablespoons of the olive oil, then add the tomatoes. Cook until they have browned slightly, then add the diced sweet peppers. Let this mixture simmer while the pasta cooks.

Cook the pasta until *al dente*, then drain.

Add the tomato paste to the vegetables, then stir in the drained pasta, the remaining chopped garlic, and the remaining olive oil.

Toss in half the goat cheese, season with oregano, salt and pepper and top with the remaining goat cheese. Serve immediately, accompanied by the grated cheese.

SERVES 4

Pasta with Puréed Red Sweet Pepper Sauce

This is one of the easiest yet most elegant sauces I know. It takes two hours to cook, but the big plus is that most of that time it simply sits in the oven, slowly baking its way to strong and delicious flavor. However, if baking for so long is impractical, it may be slowly sautéed on the stove instead.

6 red sweet peppers (capsicums), diced
2 yellow sweet peppers (capsicums), diced
3 onions, diced
3–4 ripe tomatoes, diced
10–12 garlic cloves, coarsely chopped
salt and freshly ground black pepper, to taste
2 tablespoons extra virgin olive oil
3–5 fl. oz. (90–155 ml) light (single) cream
1 lb. (500 g) fettuccine or other pasta
finely chopped fresh basil or marjoram leaves,
    to serve (optional)
freshly grated Parmesan cheese, to serve

Place the red and yellow sweet peppers, onion, tomatoes, and garlic in an earthenware casserole.

Sprinkle with salt and toss with the olive oil, then bake, uncovered, in the oven at 350°F (180°C) for 2 hours, turning once or twice. (This may be done up to two days in advance.)

Purée the vegetables in a blender or food processor, then add enough cream to form a sauce and purée together until fairly smooth. Push through a sieve to remove the stringy bits of skin. Season with salt and pepper. Keep warm.

Cook the pasta until *al dente*, then drain. Toss the pasta with the sauce. Garnish with herbs and Parmesan cheese, and serve immediately.

VARIATION

Creamy Red Sweet Pepper Bisque: This purée is the basis for a superb soup. Purée as above, using three-quarters of the vegetable mixture; sieve. Combine with 1½ cups (12 fl. oz., 375 ml) of vegetable broth (see p. 15), a pinch of fennel seeds, and the reserved vegetables. Heat until bubbles form around the edge. Serve immediately, garnished with a sprinkling of fresh basil.

SERVES 4–6

Fettuccine with Spicy Tequila-spiked Creamy Tomato Sauce

In this variation on the vodka-spiked sauces that were fashionable on the Via Veneto in Rome a few years ago, the vodka is replaced by a little tequila. When the tequila boils away it leaves in its wake a vague and pleasant vegetal flavor.

4 garlic cloves, chopped
¼ teaspoon red chili pepper flakes, or 1–2 dried
    red chili peppers, halved, seeds removed
2 tablespoons extra virgin olive oil or 1 oz.
    (30 g) butter
2 tablespoons tequila
8 ripe tomatoes, diced, or 14 oz. (435 g) tinned
    tomatoes, chopped
3 fl. oz. (90 ml) light (single) cream
salt and freshly ground black pepper, to taste
12 oz. (375 g) fresh fettuccine
freshly grated Parmesan cheese, to serve

Sauté the garlic and hot pepper in the olive oil or butter, until the garlic is fragrant and golden, but not brown. Remove from the heat and, keeping your face away from the pan, add the tequila. Do not pour it directly from the bottle as it is likely to burst into flames; pour it into a long-handled spoon or ladle first.

Return the pan to the heat and add the tomatoes. Cook over a high heat, letting the mixture flame up then cook down until the flames die and the liquid is reduced by half.

Add the cream and cook until it forms a thickened sauce (5–8 minutes), then season with salt and pepper.

Meanwhile, cook the pasta until *al dente*, then drain.

Serve with the sauce and a dusting of Parmesan cheese.

SERVES 4

LEFT ♦ *Macaroni with Roasted Green Sweet Peppers, Tomatoes, and Goat Cheese*

Spaghetti with Shredded, Basil-scented Zucchini and Cream

This is a rich and succulent dish, perfect for a first course or, in more generous portions, as a main course or even a midnight feast.

6 zucchini (courgettes)
2 onions, chopped
2 garlic cloves, chopped
1 oz. (30 g). butter
1½ cups (12 fl. oz., 375 ml) light (single) cream
3 oz. (90 g) Parmesan cheese, freshly grated
1 lb. (500 g) spaghetti
1 egg, lightly beaten
salt and freshly ground black pepper, to taste
handful of fresh basil leaves, thinly sliced, or large
   pinch of dried basil or mixed herbs, crushed
   between the fingers

Shred the zucchini on the large holes of a grater. Leave the shreds in a colander to drain for an hour if you have time. (Another trick for ridding them of excess water is to spin them briefly in a salad spinner.)

Lightly sauté the onions and garlic in the butter until they have just softened, then add the shredded zucchini. Cook for 1–2 minutes over medium to high heat, until the zucchini is half tender, half crunchy. Add the cream, increase the heat and cook until slightly thickened (5–6 minutes), then stir in half the cheese. Set aside.

Meanwhile, cook the spaghetti until *al dente*, then drain. Stir the beaten egg into the sauce, then toss this mixture with the spaghetti, letting the heat of the spaghetti thicken the sauce. If the egg does not cook from the heat of the pasta alone, place it over a medium heat for a few minutes, stirring all the time, until it thickens.

Season with salt, pepper, and the basil or herbs, then serve immediately, sprinkled with the remaining Parmesan cheese.

SERVES 4–6

RIGHT ♦ *Spaghetti with Shredded, Basil-scented Zucchini and Cream*

Fettuccine alla Perugina (Fettuccine with Fresh Tomato and Asparagus Sauce)

The medieval town of Perugia in Umbria is known for several culinary reasons: silken chocolate baci (kisses), of course, and black truffles nearly as good as those in France. But come the asparagus season, when the thin green shoots are in abundant supply, fresh and grassy tasting, asparagus is tossed into every dish imaginable, especially this pasta dish. Like many wonderful foods, its simplicity belies its superlative flavor. It is simply a zesty tomato sauce in which a generous amount of asparagus has been simmered, ladled over pasta and sprinkled abundantly with fresh herbs. Any large pasta, especially the long, flat, ribbony shapes such as fettuccine, linguini and even spaghetti, is delicious with this sauce. Curly pastas such as fusilli lunghi are good too.

4 garlic cloves, chopped
2 tablespoons extra virgin olive oil
12–15 small fresh tomatoes, preferably Italian,
   peeled, seeded, and diced
3 tablespoons tomato paste (purée)
1 cup (8 fl. oz., 250 ml) water
salt and freshly ground black pepper, to taste
pinch of sugar (optional)
12–16 oz. (375–500 g) asparagus, cut into
   1½–2 in. (5–7.5 cm) lengths
12 oz. (375 g) fettuccine or pasta of choice
10–15 fresh basil leaves, coarsely chopped or torn
   (or chopped parsley, marjoram, etc.)
2–3 tablespoons freshly grated Parmesan cheese,
   to serve

Heat the garlic in the olive oil until just warmed and fragrant, then add the tomatoes and sauté until softened. This will take about 5 minutes. Add the tomato paste and water, season with salt and pepper and the sugar, if needed, then add the asparagus.

Bring the sauce to the boil, then reduce the heat and cook until the asparagus is just tender.

Meanwhile, cook the pasta until *al dente*, then drain.

Toss the cooked pasta with the sauce and top with the basil and grated Parmesan cheese. Serve immediately.

SERVES 4–6

Paglia e Fieno al Aurora (Yellow and Green Pasta in a Creamy Tomato Sauce with Mushrooms and Peas)

Paglia e fieno means straw and hay, and it is a whimsical term for yellow and green pasta, reminiscent of the yellow hay stacks and green piles of straw that are so much a part of the Tuscan landscape.

1 small onion, chopped
4 garlic cloves, chopped
8 oz. (250 g) mushrooms, coarsely chopped
1 oz. (30 g) butter
1½ lbs. (750 g) ripe tomatoes, peeled and chopped, or 14 oz. (435 g) tinned tomatoes, chopped
1 oz. (30 g) tomato paste (purée)
1 cup (8 fl. oz., 250 ml) vegetable broth (see p. 15)
1 cup (8 fl. oz., 250 ml) light (single) cream
8 oz. (250 g) fresh and blanched, or frozen peas
salt and freshly ground black pepper, to taste
8 oz. (250 g) yellow fettuccine
8 oz. (250 g) green fettuccine
handful of fresh basil leaves, cut into strips, or several tablespoons coarsely chopped fresh marjoram
freshly grated Parmesan cheese, to serve

Lightly sauté the onion, garlic, and mushrooms in the butter until they have just softened. Add the tomatoes, tomato paste, and broth, then cook over a medium heat for 5–10 minutes, until the mixture is thick and sauce-like.

Stir in the cream and cook for another 10 minutes, or until the sauce has thickened again, and the flavors have combined. Add the peas, then season with salt and pepper.

Meanwhile, cook the pasta until *al dente*. Drain and serve immediately, tossed with the sauce and sprinkled with the basil or marjoram. Offer Parmesan separately.

VARIATION
Instead of peas, add a handful of thin green beans, blanched and cut into bite-sized lengths. If yellow wax beans are available, include these as well.

SERVES 4–6

LEFT ♦ *Paglia e Fieno al Aurora (Yellow and Green Pasta in a Creamy Tomato Sauce with Mushrooms and Peas)*

Orzo with Peas in Saffron and Garlic Cream

Tiny pasta in saffron- and garlic-scented cream makes a succulent first course or supper dish to spoon up any time when you are leaning towards indulgence.

12 oz. (375 g) orzo or other small seed-shaped pasta
6 garlic cloves, chopped
1½ oz. (45 g) butter
2 cups (16 fl. oz., 500 ml) vegetable broth (see p. 15)
¾ cup (6 fl. oz., 185 ml) light (single) cream
½ cup (4 fl. oz., 125 ml) Greek-style yogurt or crème frâiche or sour cream
8 oz. (250 g) peas, preferably petits pois, either fresh and blanched, or frozen
large pinch of saffron dissolved in 1 tablespoon cold water
3 oz. (90 g) freshly grated Parmesan cheese, to serve

Cook the orzo in boiling, salted water until *al dente*. Drain and set aside.

Lightly heat the garlic in the butter until it is just fragrant. Add the broth and the cooked orzo. Heat until bubbly around the edges.

Stir in the cream, then add the yogurt or crème frâiche or sour cream, peas, and saffron. Heat the sauce, stirring well until it is smooth and creamy — it should be soupy, but thickened.

Serve immediately, topping each portion with a sprinkling of Parmesan cheese.

VARIATIONS
Orzo with Asparagus and Saffron and Garlic Cream: Instead of the tiny peas, use asparagus tips, cut into bite-sized pieces. Cook the asparagus with the orzo, adding it when the pasta is half done. Then proceed as above, omitting the peas.

Orzo with Zucchini Blossoms: A variation on the classic pairing of squash blossoms with pasta or arborio rice. Clean about 15 zucchini (courgette) flowers or other squash blossoms; remove the stems and pistils. Cut into large pieces and add to the orzo instead of the peas.

SERVES 4

Pasta Arrabbiata
(Pasta with Chili-spiked Tomato Sauce)

A good arrabbiata sauce can either grab your throat with its fiery heat or merely warm you gently, whatever you prefer. It should also, to my taste at least, fairly reek with garlic. The spicy character of the sauce makes a delicious foil to other additions: sun-dried tomatoes, fresh basil leaves, goat cheese, slices of browned eggplant (aubergine), chopped arugula (rocket) or spinach.

1–2 dried red chili peppers, crumbled, or cayenne pepper, to taste
4–6 garlic cloves, chopped
2–3 tablespoons extra virgin olive oil
1 cup (8 fl. oz., 250 ml) tomato purée (passata)
salt and freshly ground black pepper, to taste
12 oz. (375 g) pasta of choice: vermicelli, fettuccine, spaghetti, bucatini, etc.
3 tablespoons chopped fresh parsley
freshly grated Parmesan cheese, to serve (optional)

Warm the chili peppers or cayenne pepper and garlic in the olive oil until the garlic is fragrant. As always, when heating chili peppers in oil, take care not to inhale the irritating fumes.

Add the tomato purée; season with salt and pepper. Cook the sauce for 5–10 minutes, to meld the flavors.

Cook the pasta until *al dente*, then drain.

Serve the pasta tossed with the sauce and sprinkled with the parsley, and offer Parmesan separately.

VARIATIONS

Pasta Arrabbiata with Ginger–Garlic Butter, Lemon, and Mint: Prepare as above, but serve topped with a nugget of ginger–garlic butter, sprinkled with 1–2 tablespoons each of chopped fresh mint and parsley, and accompanied by lemon wedges.

To make ginger-garlic butter, mix 2 oz. (60 g) of softened unsalted butter with ½–1 teaspoon of grated fresh ginger, 1 garlic clove (chopped), and a pinch of salt.

Pasta Arrabbiata with Coriander Pesto: To make coriander pesto, mix the following ingredients in a blender or food processor: 3 garlic cloves, chopped, 1 bunch of fresh coriander leaves, also chopped, 2–3 oz. (60–90 g) Parmesan or other hard cheese, coarsely grated, 2–3 tablespoons extra virgin olive oil, and salt and freshly ground black pepper or cayenne pepper, to taste. Serve the sauced pasta with a generous dab of coriander pesto.

SERVES 4

Roasted Tomato and Green Bean
Couscous with Ginger

This couscous has Italian flavors, reminiscent of Sicilian couscous rather than the highly spiced affairs of Morocco and Tunisia. It makes a particularly good side dish for grilled vegetable kebabs, especially with a salad of slightly bitter frisée (curly endive) leaves.

3 garlic cloves, chopped
2 tablespoons extra virgin olive oil
6–8 tomatoes, roasted, peeled and diced (see p. 18)
8 oz. (250 g) green or string beans, fresh and blanched, or frozen, cut into bite-sized lengths
2½ cups (1 imp. pint, 625 ml) vegetable broth (see p. 15), plus extra, if needed
12 oz. (375 g) instant couscous
½ teaspoon powdered ginger, or to taste
dash of Tabasco sauce or pinch of cayenne pepper
salt, to taste

Sauté the garlic in the olive oil then add the roasted tomatoes and beans, and cook for a few moments.

Add the broth and bring to the boil, then add the couscous. Remove from the heat, cover and leave for 5 minutes, then make sure the mixture is still moist. If it is not moist enough, add more broth. Leave for another 5 minutes.

Add the ginger, then reheat the couscous, and season with Tabasco sauce or cayenne pepper and salt. Serve immediately.

SERVES 4–6

RIGHT ♦ *Pasta Arrabbiata (Pasta with Chili-spiked Tomato Sauce)*

Pasta with Sage Sauce

Potent sage purée is mellowed with a little broth and enriched with a small amount of butter. Sometimes I omit the broth and serve the buttered, sage-dressed pasta sprinkled with Parmesan cheese or tossed with a little tangy, soft goat cheese. Wide pastas such as pappardelle or lasagne are good with this; stuffed pastas are better still. I often serve the sage-dressed pasta tossed with diced ripe tomatoes, or with diced cooked beets (beetroot) and a drizzle of their scarlet juice.

2 garlic cloves, chopped
1 fl. oz. (30 ml) extra virgin olive oil
small handful of fresh sage leaves, finely chopped
12 oz. (375 g) wide pasta of choice, or stuffed pasta
1 oz. (30 g) unsalted butter
2 tablespoons vegetable broth (see p. 15)
coarsely chopped fresh parsley, preferably flat-leaf
   (Italian), to serve

Process the garlic, olive oil, and sage in a blender or food processor or pound in a mortar and pestle until it becomes a pungent, bright green balm. It doesn't need to be smooth; small bits of sage add welcome texture.

Cook the pasta until *al dente*, then drain. Toss the pasta with the butter, broth, and sage sauce, then serve immediately, sprinkled with parsley.

SERVES 4

Rotelle, Penne, or Rigatoni with Tomato Sauce, Broccoli, and Ricotta Cheese

Robust, chewy pasta, served up with fennel-scented tomato sauce, punctuated with nuggets of broccoli and dollops of snowy ricotta cheese.

4–6 garlic cloves, chopped
2 small onions, chopped
1 small carrot, diced
1 small celery stalk, chopped
2 tablespoons extra virgin olive oil
1½ teaspoons fennel seeds
1 teaspoon fresh thyme or ½ teaspoon dried thyme, crushed
pinch of dried marjoram, crushed (optional)
1½ lbs. (750 g) ripe tomatoes, chopped, or 1½ tins (14 oz., 435 g tins) chopped tomatoes
1 small tin tomato purée (passata)
pinch of sugar
2 tablespoons coarsely chopped fresh rosemary or 3 tablespoons thinly sliced fresh basil leaves
1 lb. (500 g) rotelle, penne, or rigatoni
2 heads broccoli, cut into bite-sized florets
8 oz. (250 g) fresh ricotta cheese
freshly grated Parmesan, pecorino, aged Asiago, or other grating cheese, to serve
salt and freshly ground black pepper, to taste

Sauté the garlic, onion, carrot, and celery in the olive oil until they have softened, then add the fennel seeds, thyme, marjoram (if using), tomatoes, tomato purée, and sugar. Bring to the boil, then reduce the heat, and simmer uncovered for about 10 minutes, until the sauce is thick and flavorful. Remove from the heat and add the rosemary or basil.

Cook the pasta until half-done, then add the broccoli. Continue cooking until both are *al dente,* then drain.

Toss the broccoli and pasta with the sauce, then top each portion with a generous dollop of ricotta and a sprinkling of grated cheese. Season with salt and pepper, if needed, and serve immediately.

SERVES 4–6

LEFT ♦ *Rotelle, Penne, or Rigatoni with Tomato Sauce, Broccoli, and Ricotta Cheese*

Lumache or Penne with Creamy Spinach and Ricotta Sauce

Scallions (spring onions) add fresh flavor to this creamy spinach sauce. If the sauce becomes too rich and thick, thin it with a little water or milk.

8 oz. (250 g) fresh spinach or 6 oz. (185 g) frozen spinach
2 scallions (spring onions), chopped
1 garlic clove, chopped
1 oz. (30 g) butter
1 tablespoon flour
1 cup (8 fl. oz., 250 ml) hot (not boiling) milk
8 oz. (250 g) ricotta cheese or fromage frais
1½ oz. (45 g) Parmesan cheese, freshly grated
large pinch of dried mixed herbs or 1 tablespoon chopped fresh basil
small pinch of freshly grated nutmeg
salt and freshly ground black pepper, to taste
12 oz. (375 g) lumache or penne

Cook the spinach in boiling water until bright green and tender. Rinse in cold water and squeeze dry. Chop coarsely and set aside.

Lightly sauté the scallions and garlic in the butter. When they are soft, sprinkle the flour over and stir until it is cooked through (2–3 minutes). Remove the pan from the heat, stir in the milk, then return to the heat and stir until the mixture thickens. Add the spinach and heat for a minute or two, then stir in the ricotta or fromage frais, Parmesan cheese, mixed herbs, nutmeg, and salt and pepper. Set aside and keep warm while you cook the pasta.

Cook the pasta until *al dente,* then drain. Toss the pasta with the hot sauce. Serve immediately, sprinkled with more Parmesan cheese.

VARIATION

Add about 10 diced or sliced sun-dried tomatoes to the spinach sauce. If you are using dried ones, cook them with the pasta; if you are using oil-marinated ones, add them to the sauce with the spinach.

SERVES 4–6

Conchiglie with Yellow Sweet Peppers and Eggplant Sauce

This dish is inspired by the myriad sun-drenched pasta and vegetable dishes I've eaten in Italy. You can, of course, vary the vegetables: add zucchini (courgettes) and you will have a ratatouille-like sauce; red sweet pepper (capsicum) instead of yellow, or diced fennel, will give yet another effect.

1 onion, coarsely chopped
4 garlic cloves, coarsely chopped
1 yellow sweet pepper (capsicum), diced
6 tablespoons extra virgin olive oil
1 eggplant (aubergine), cut into bite-sized cubes
6 small to medium ripe tomatoes, diced, or
   14 oz. (435 g) tinned tomatoes, chopped
salt and freshly ground black pepper, to taste
pinch of sugar (optional)
1 teaspoon fresh or ½ teaspoon dried oregano
   or marjoram

12 oz. (375 g) conchiglie (pasta shells)
4 oz. (125 g) green or string beans, cut into
   bite-sized lengths
4 tablespoons freshly grated Parmesan cheese

Sauté the onion, garlic, and sweet pepper in about half the olive oil until they are soft, then remove them from the pan. Add the remaining olive oil and brown the eggplant. Remove from the pan and set aside.

Cook the tomatoes in the pan, adding a little more oil if necessary. When the mixture has the consistency of a sauce, return the vegetables to the pan. Season with salt and pepper, the sugar (if using), and the oregano or marjoram. Set aside.

Cook the pasta until about half-done, then add the beans and continue cooking until both are *al dente*.

Drain and mix with the sauce. Toss with the cheese and serve immediately.

SERVES 4–6

Fusilli Siracusani
(Sicilian Eggplant Pasta)

Diced eggplant (aubergine), roasted sweet peppers (capsicums), tomatoes, and lots of black olives and capers season this garlicky, basil-scented tomato sauce that clings to the fat curly strands of the pasta known as fusilli lunghi. Spaghetti is also delicious in this Sicilian dish.

1 red sweet pepper (capsicum)
1 yellow sweet pepper (capsicum)
1 eggplant (aubergine), cut into bite-sized pieces
extra virgin olive oil for sautéing
5 garlic cloves, chopped
1 onion, thinly sliced
2 lbs. (1 kg) ripe tomatoes, diced, or 2 tins
   (14 oz., 435 g tins) chopped tomatoes
pinch of sugar (optional)
4 tablespoons tomato paste (purée)
15 black olives (Greek, Gaeta, kalamata, or
   oil-cured), pitted and diced
2 tablespoons capers
dash of balsamic vinegar (optional)
salt and freshly ground black pepper, to taste
1 lb. (500 g) fusilli lunghi or spaghetti
handful of fresh basil leaves, torn or coarsely chopped
freshly grated Parmesan cheese, to serve

Roast the sweet peppers (see p. 19), then cut them into strips. Set aside.

Brown the eggplant, using as little olive oil as possible, to avoid greasiness. (You may salt, rinse, and drain, then dry it before browning.) Add the garlic and set aside.

Lightly brown the onions in a little olive oil, then add the tomatoes and sugar (if using) and cook over a medium heat for about 15 minutes, or until the mixture has the consistency of a sauce.

Add the sweet peppers, the eggplant and garlic, and the tomato paste. Cook for another 15 minutes, or until the eggplant is tender, then add the olives and capers, plus the balsamic vinegar (if using). Season with salt and pepper.

Cook the pasta until *al dente;* drain. Toss with the sauce and the fresh basil. Serve with Parmesan cheese as desired.

SERVES 4–6

LEFT ♦ *Conchiglie with Yellow Sweet Peppers and Eggplant Sauce*

Pasta with Tomato Sauce,
Beaten Egg, Cheese, and Basil

The addition of beaten egg and cheese makes a simple tomato sauce softer and smoother. I've tried it both ways: tossing the pasta with the sauce first, then with the beaten egg, and tossing the pasta with egg and cheese, carbonara-style, then adding the tomato sauce. Each gives a slightly different result. It is best to make this dish using a wide skillet (frying pan), as the larger cooking surface will evaporate the liquids and intensify the flavor of the sauce more quickly.

2 onions, chopped
2½ oz. (75 g) butter
4 garlic cloves, coarsely chopped
2 lbs. (1 kg) very ripe tomatoes, peeled, seeded and
   diced, or 1½ tins (14 oz., 435 g tins) tomatoes,
   drained and sliced (reserve the juice)
salt and freshly ground black pepper, to taste
pinch of sugar
1 lb. (500 g) pasta of choice: spaghetti, tiny shells,
   elbows, etc.
3 eggs, lightly beaten
3 oz. (90 g) Parmesan cheese, freshly grated
4 oz. (125 g) mozzarella, Jack, or similar cheese,
   grated
about 10 fresh basil leaves, cut into very thin strips

In a wide skillet or frying pan, lightly sauté the onions in 3 tablespoons of the butter until they are soft, then add the garlic and continue to cook for a minute or so.

Add the tomatoes, season with salt and pepper, and sugar, and cook over medium to high heat until the liquid is nearly evaporated. Add about ½ cup (4 fl. oz., 125 ml) of the reserved juice, adjust the seasoning if necessary, and set aside to keep warm.

Meanwhile, cook the pasta until *al dente.* Combine the beaten eggs with the Parmesan and mozzarella (or Jack) cheeses.

Drain the pasta and mix it with the remaining butter. Season with pepper. Toss the buttered pasta with the egg and cheese mixture, taking care that it forms a creamy cloak rather than becoming scrambled.

Once the cheese has melted, stir the tomato sauce through. Serve immediately, garnished with the basil.

SERVES 4–6

Greek-flavored Lemon Orzo with Yogurt–Vegetable Topping

Delicious as a side dish, especially alongside a Mediterranean-style tomato and eggplant (aubergine) stew. The orzo may be prepared up to an hour in advance. You may need to add a few spoonfuls of water when you reheat over a medium flame, and a little more lemon juice just before serving.

12 oz. (375 g) orzo
1½ oz. (45 g) butter
1 egg, lightly beaten
finely grated rind and juice of 1 lemon, more if needed
salt and freshly ground black pepper, to taste
pinch of dried mint (optional)
2 tablespoons coarsely chopped fresh parsley, preferably flat-leaf (Italian)
2 garlic cloves, chopped
1 cup (8 fl. oz., 250 ml) Greek-style yogurt, preferably sheep's milk
1 small green sweet pepper (capsicum), diced
1 small onion, coarsely chopped
1 teaspoon paprika

Cook the orzo until *al dente*, then drain. Toss the pasta with the butter.

Mix the egg and the lemon rind and juice together, then toss with the hot buttered orzo, taking care that it mixes into a creamy pasta rather than into scrambled eggs. Season with salt and pepper, the mint, parsley, and half the garlic.

Combine the yogurt, sweet pepper, onion, and remaining garlic in a serving bowl and sprinkle with the paprika.

Serve each portion of creamy, tangy orzo topped with a spoonful of the yogurt mixture.

SERVES 4

Orzo with Greek Island Flavors

This is a variation of a dish I enjoyed time and again during a winter on a Greek island. It has all the hallmark Greek flavors: tomatoes, cinnamon and allspice, onions and garlic, along with the tangy nip of feta cheese. I was surprised, therefore, when a friend from the Sudan exclaimed that she ate this all the time at home. Her version was much simplified, however, and used spaghetti rather than orzo.

1 onion, coarsely chopped
4 garlic cloves, chopped
3 tablespoons extra virgin olive oil
1 cup (8 fl. oz., 250 ml) tomato purée (passata)
8 oz. (250 g) diced tomatoes (either fresh or tinned)
pinch of cinnamon
pinch of allspice or cloves
pinch of sugar (optional)
1 bunch fresh spinach, cooked and coarsely chopped, or 12 oz. (375 g) frozen spinach, defrosted
¼ teaspoon dried oregano
12 oz. (375 g) orzo
4 oz. (125 g) feta cheese, coarsely crumbled
chopped fresh parsley (optional)
salt and freshly ground black pepper, to taste

Lightly sauté the onion and garlic in the olive oil until they are softened, then add the tomato purée and tomatoes. Bring to the boil; season with the cinnamon, allspice or cloves, and sugar (if needed), then add the spinach. Simmer over a medium heat until the mixture is reduced in volume and flavorful. Season with the oregano and set aside.

Meanwhile, cook the orzo until it is half-tender, then drain. Add to the tomato and spinach mixture. Simmer together until the orzo is tender.

Toss the sauced pasta with three-quarters of the feta cheese and sprinkle with the rest, then with the parsley (if using). Check the seasoning, adding more cinnamon, oregano, and salt and pepper, if needed. Serve immediately.

SERVES 4–6

Spaghetti alla Norma

This comes from Sicily, where pasta and eggplant (aubergine) dishes, usually bearing the name Norma, abound. The name is a reference to the opera Norma, *by the composer Bellini, who was born in Sicily. The opera was such a resounding success that 'Norma' became a term of excellence, and eventually was used to describe Sicily's eggplant and pasta dishes. While the name can refer to nearly any combination of the two, this simple dish is my favorite: a mound of pasta topped with tomato sauce and fresh herbs, and surrounded by a border of browned eggplant slices.*
In Sicily this can be nearly instant fare: ready-fried eggplants are sold in the markets, so all you really have to do at home is boil the spaghetti and make the simple sauce. Ricotta salata, salted ricotta that is aged and firm enough for grating, is the authentic cheese for this dish; if you can, use it in place of the more easily available Parmesan.

2 large eggplants (aubergines), cut into ⅛–¼ in.
   (3–6 mm) slices
salt
extra virgin olive oil
1 onion, chopped
3 garlic cloves, chopped
pinch of sugar
2½ cups (1 imp. pint, 625 ml) tomato purée
   (passata), or 2 lbs. (500 g) ripe tomatoes, diced,
   or 2 tins (14 oz., 435 g tins) chopped tomatoes
freshly ground black pepper, to taste
1 lb. (500 g) spaghetti
freshly grated ricotta salata cheese, or Parmesan,
   or pecorino, to serve
handful of fresh herbs: basil, parsley, oregano,
   thyme, marjoram, etc.

Sprinkle the eggplant liberally with salt, and leave for at least an hour. Rinse and pat dry with a clean towel or absorbent paper.

Brown the eggplant in a heavy skillet (frying pan) in olive oil, taking care not to crowd the pan, and cooking only one layer at a time. (The eggplant can be lightly dredged in flour to prevent it absorbing too much oil; I like the flavor of the eggplant rather than a floury crust, but the choice is yours.) Place the browned eggplant slices on a flat baking sheet (tray) and set aside.

Prepare the sauce by sautéing the onions and garlic in about 2 tablespoons of olive oil, until they have just softened. Add the sugar and tomato purée or tomatoes. Season with pepper and simmer for 15 minutes, or until full-flavored. Keep warm.

Cook the spaghetti until *al dente*; at the same time, reheat the eggplant slices in a medium hot oven.

Drain the spaghetti and place it on a platter. Arrange a ring of eggplant slices around the spaghetti, then ladle the tomato sauce over the pasta. Serve immediately, sprinkled generously with cheese and fresh herbs.

SERVES 4–6

Melissa's Spaghetti

My young niece, Melissa, is mad about celery. Because of her passion, I have become reacquainted with this often-overlooked vegetable, and very fond of this Tuscan pasta dish. The fiery heat makes a splendid contrast to the fresh, light celery. It is an unusual dish, and very simple to prepare.

1 head celery, stalks cut into short batons
6–8 garlic cloves, coarsely chopped
3–4 tablespoons extra virgin olive oil
1 dried hot red chili pepper, or more, to taste
salt
1 lb. (500 g) spaghetti

Blanch the celery in a large pan of boiling water, then remove with a slotted spoon, leaving the celery-scented water for cooking the pasta in.

Sauté the garlic and blanched celery in the olive oil with the hot chili pepper until they are a light golden brown. Remove the hot chili pepper and season the garlic and celery with salt.

Cook the spaghetti in the celery water until *al dente*, then drain and toss with the garlic and celery mixture, adding more salt if needed.

VARIATION
Breadcrumbs, either fresh or toasted, add crispy texture to the dish for a delicious variation. Sprinkle over a tablespoon or two per person.

SERVES 4–6

Pasta with Eggplant and Tomato Sauce

A savory sauce of tomatoes simmered with red wine and chunks of sautéed eggplant (aubergine), then tossed with pasta and mozzarella cheese until the cheese is just warm and softened.

1 large or 2 small eggplants (aubergines), cut into large dice
several tablespoons of extra virgin olive oil
1 onion, diced
3 garlic cloves, chopped
1½ cups (12 fl. oz., 375 ml) tomato purée (passata)
½–¾ cup (4–6 fl. oz., 125–185 ml) dry red wine
pinch of sugar (optional)
salt and freshly ground black pepper, to taste
large pinch of dried oregano, crushed between the fingers
12-16 oz. (375-500 g) spaghetti, fusilli, rigatoni, or other hearty pasta shape
8 oz. (250 g) mozzarella cheese (a firm one, for slicing) or other mild white cheese, cut into bite-sized pieces

Sauté the eggplant in olive oil until it is light brown. Remove from the pan and set aside. (The eggplant may be salted, rinsed and drained before browning to remove any bitterness and prevent it absorbing excess oil.)

In the same pan, lightly sauté the onion and garlic in about 1 tablespoon of olive oil until they have softened, then add the tomato purée and red wine. Bring to the boil, then reduce the heat and simmer for 15–20 minutes, or until richly flavored. Season with sugar (if needed), salt and pepper, and oregano.

Return the browned eggplant to the sauce and continue to simmer while the pasta cooks.

Cook the pasta until *al dente*, then drain.

Toss the pasta with the sauce to mix well, then add the cheese. Serve immediately.

SERVES 6

Farfalle with Creamy Tarragon and Shredded Mushroom Sauce

Shredding the mushrooms brings out their foresty flavor, producing an almost truffle-like effect. The shredded mushrooms are added to a tarragon-scented béchamel, along with lots of Parmesan cheese, then tossed with farfalle. This is an unusual pasta dish with a French flavor.

1½ oz. (45 g) butter
1 tablespoon flour
1 cup (8 fl. oz., 250 ml) hot (not boiling) milk
12 oz. (375 g) farfalle or similar pasta shape
12 oz. (375 g) mushrooms, coarsely shredded on the large holes of a grater
generous pinch of dried tarragon or 1–2 teaspoons fresh chopped tarragon
1½ oz. (45 g) Parmesan cheese, freshly grated
salt and freshly ground black pepper, to taste

Melt one-third of the butter and sprinkle with the flour. Cook for a minute or so without stirring, then remove from the heat and whisk in the milk. Return to the heat, whisking or stirring, and cook until the mixture thickens. Set aside and keep warm.

Cook the pasta until *al dente*, then drain.

Meanwhile, quickly brown the mushrooms in the remaining butter. Add the sauce to the mushrooms, heat through, then season with the tarragon and stir in the Parmesan cheese.

Toss the pasta with the sauce, season with salt and pepper, and serve.

VARIATION

Pasta Soufflé: For a soufflé-like baked variation, add 4 egg yolks to the sauce, then whip the whites up until stiff and fold into the sauce. Fold half the sauce into cooked pasta such as fettuccine, pour the mixture into a soufflé dish, top with remaining sauce, then bake in the oven at 425°F (220°C) until the soufflé is well risen and the top is golden brown.

SERVES 4

RIGHT ♦ *Pasta with Eggplant and Tomato Sauce*

Pasta with Asparagus and Creamy Light Pesto Sauce

The creamy pale green sauce, subtly scented with basil, and the delicate asparagus go particularly well with fresh pasta in this dish.

12–16 oz. (375–500 g) good-quality fresh flat ribbon pasta

12 oz. (375 g) fresh asparagus, cut into 2-in. (5-cm) lengths

4 oz. (125 g) pesto (see p. 16) (bottled pesto doesn't taste right here)

1 ½ oz. (45 g) unsalted butter, softened
½ cup (4 fl. oz./125 ml) light (single) cream
1 garlic clove, finely chopped
salt and freshly ground black pepper, to taste

Cook the pasta and asparagus together in boiling salted water until the pasta is *al dente* and the asparagus is crisp-tender, about 3 minutes; drain.

Mix the pesto with the butter, cream, and garlic. Season with salt and pepper.

Toss the hot pasta and asparagus with the creamy pesto mixture and serve immediately.

SERVES 4–6

Fettuccine with Yellow and Red Sweet Peppers in Garlicky Cream Sauce

Strips of roasted yellow and red sweet pepper (capsicum) awash with garlic-scented cream, served over supple, chewy fettuccine. Blanket it with lots of freshly grated Parmesan, and serve in bowls, as a first course, followed by a sauté of asparagus and strongly flavored mushrooms.

2 red sweet peppers (capsicums)
2 yellow sweet peppers (capsicums)
1½ oz. (45 g) butter
4–6 garlic cloves, chopped
½ cup (4 fl. oz., 125 ml) dry white wine
1½ cups (12 fl. oz., 375 ml) light (single) cream
12–16 oz. (375–500 g) fettuccine
handful of fresh basil leaves, coarsely shredded
a generous amount of freshly grated Parmesan
    cheese, to serve
freshly ground black pepper, to taste

Roast the sweet peppers (see p. 19), then slice them into thin strips. Set aside.

Heat the butter gently and warm the garlic in it. Add the sweet peppers, then pour in the wine, and increase the heat. Cook over a high heat until the wine is reduced to a thickened, almost syrupy essence, then add the cream. Reduce the heat and cook the sauce until it has thickened, then remove from the heat, cover, and keep warm.

Meanwhile, cook the pasta until *al dente*, then drain. Toss the pasta with the sauce and the basil.

Serve in shallow bowls, each portion blanketed with fresh Parmesan cheese. Pass the peppermill and a chunk of Parmesan (along with a grater) for those who would like more cheese.

SERVES 4–6

ABOVE ♦ *Fettuccine with Yellow and Red Sweet Peppers in Garlicky Cream Sauce*
LEFT ♦ *Pasta with Asparagus and Creamy Light Pesto Sauce*

Pasta with Pungent Greens and Cherry Tomatoes

1½ lbs. (750 g) greens — turnip tops, cabbage greens, dandelion greens, beet (beetroot) greens, broccoli tops, broccoli, spinach, or a combination
1 lb. (500 g) orecchiette
4 tablespoons extra virgin olive oil
3 garlic cloves, chopped
15–20 cherry tomatoes, halved
salt and freshly ground black pepper or cayenne pepper, to taste
freshly grated or shaved Parmesan cheese, to serve

Cook the greens in boiling salted water for about 5 minutes. Add the pasta and cook until *al dente,* then drain. Toss the pasta with 1 tablespoon of the olive oil.

Meanwhile, heat the remaining olive oil and the garlic, then quickly sauté the tomatoes over medium to high heat for 3–5 minutes.

Combine the pasta and greens with the sautéed tomatoes and serve immediately, seasoned well with salt and either black pepper or cayenne pepper, and tossed with Parmesan cheese.

VARIATIONS

Instead of fresh tomatoes, tomato purée (passata) may be used. Sprinkle with parsley along with the cheese.
Orecchiette with Cherry Tomatoes, Celery, and Garlic Croûtons: Omit the greens and sauté 1 chopped onion and 1 chopped celery stalk with the garlic, then add the cherry tomatoes. To make garlic croûtons, brown 1 thick slice of French or Italian-style bread, diced, in a tablespoon or so of olive oil. When croûtons are golden, remove from heat and add one garlic clove, chopped. Toss the orecchiette in the celery and tomato sauce, then serve topped with garlic croûtons.

SERVES 4–6

Sardinian-inspired Pasta with Tomato Sauce and Mint-seasoned Ricotta Cheese

Sardinians often use ricotta seasoned with fresh mint for stuffing ravioli. Here, I've used the mixture as a topping for a zesty tomato-sauced pasta. Fresh mint adds a fragrant freshness to the bland ricotta, and a sprinkling of Parmesan or pecorino cheese gives it all a salty tang.

2 small to medium onions, coarsely chopped
4 garlic cloves, coarsely chopped
1 celery stalk, diced
2 tablespoons chopped fresh parsley
2–3 tablespoons extra virgin olive oil
2½–3½ cups (1–1½ imp. pints, 625–900 ml) tomato purée (passata)
pinch of sugar (optional)
salt and freshly ground black pepper, to taste
large pinch of oregano leaves, crumbled
8 oz. (250 g) ricotta cheese
2 teaspoons chopped fresh mint leaves, preferably small peppermint or Corsican mint
12–16 oz. (375–500 g) pasta: choose a chewy, dense shape such as gemelli, fusilli, orecchiette, small elbows, etc.

Lightly sauté the onions, garlic, celery, and parsley in the olive oil until the onions have softened, then add the tomato purée, sugar (if using), salt and pepper, and oregano. Bring to the boil, then reduce the heat and simmer for 5–10 minutes.

Meanwhile, combine the ricotta with the mint and set aside.

Cook the pasta until *al dente,* then drain.

Serve the pasta tossed with the tomato sauce and topped with dollops of the mint-seasoned ricotta.

SERVES 4–6

RIGHT ♦ *Pasta with Pungent Greens and Cherry Tomatoes*

Fettuccine with Broccoli, Spinach, and Carrot Butter

1 lb. (500 g) spinach leaves
10–12 oz. (310–375 g) broccoli, cut into florets,
   the stems peeled and sliced
4 young carrots
½ cup (4 fl. oz., 125 ml) dry white wine
½ cup (4 fl. oz., 125 ml) vegetable broth
   (see p. 15)
4–5 shallots, chopped
2 garlic cloves, chopped
pinch of tarragon
4 tablespoons butter, cut into 6–8 pieces
12 oz. (375 g) fettuccine, preferably fresh

Steam the spinach until it is just bright green. Remove from the heat and leave to cool. Squeeze out the excess liquid and chop into bite-sized pieces.

Steam the broccoli until bright green and still crunchy, then remove from the steamer and set aside with the spinach.

Dice two of the carrots and place in a small pan with the wine, broth, shallots, garlic, and tarragon. Bring to the boil, cover, and cook until the carrots are tender (6–8 minutes). Remove the cover and boil until the liquid is reduced to about 2 tablespoons. Remove from the heat.

Mash the cooked carrots with their liquid, using a fork or a food processor. When the mixture cools to just warm, whisk in the chunks of butter, one or two at a time, letting it combine into a creamy sauce before adding more. Set aside.

Grate the remaining carrots.

Cook the pasta until *al dente,* then drain. Toss the pasta with the spinach and broccoli, then spoon on the carrot butter. Serve immediately, sprinkled with the grated carrots.

SERVES 4–6

Pasta with Zucchini, Beaten Egg, and Cheese

This is typical southern Italian fare, based on what is at hand. In the summer this means lots of zucchini (courgettes), as anyone who has ever grown them in a sunny climate will tell you.

12 oz. (375 g) tubular pasta such as ziti, penne, elbow pasta, etc.
2 medium sized zucchini (courgettes), cut into ½-in. (1-cm) dice
6–10 garlic cloves, chopped
2 tablespoons extra virgin olive oil
2 eggs, lightly beaten
2 oz. (60 g) Parmesan cheese, freshly grated
salt and freshly ground black pepper, to taste

Cook the pasta until half-done, then add the zucchini. Continue cooking until the pasta and the zucchini are *al dente*, then drain.

Meanwhile, heat the garlic (but do not brown it) in the olive oil.

Toss the drained pasta and zucchini in this garlic–olive oil mixture, then toss with the beaten eggs, then with the cheese.

Season with pepper (and salt, if needed), and serve immediately.

VARIATION
Pasta with Sautéed Zucchini, Mozzarella Cheese, and Egg: Slice (rather than dice) the zucchini and sauté with the garlic in the olive oil instead of cooking it with the pasta. Toss the sautéed zucchini with the cooked pasta, beaten eggs and Parmesan, then add about 8 oz. (250 g) of mozzarella cheese (the firm kind, not the soft, fresh, milky kind), diced, and toss together until the cheese softens and melts.

SERVES 4

Pasta with Tomato and Zucchini Sauce

While zucchini (courgettes) are usually at their best when cooked only lightly, in this traditional sauce they are simmered until they softly fall apart.

3–5 garlic cloves, chopped
2 tablespoons extra virgin olive oil
1 cup (8 fl. oz., 250 ml) tomato purée (passata)
3–4 small to medium zucchini (courgettes), cut into bite-sized chunks
12 oz. (375 g) pasta of choice such as fettuccine, spaghetti, etc.
freshly grated Parmesan cheese, to serve
chopped fresh parsley, basil, thyme or other herbs of choice, to serve

Lightly sauté the garlic in the olive oil until it is fragrant but not browned. Add the tomato purée and zucchini. Cover and simmer until the zucchini are falling apart (10–15 minutes), adding water or a little vegetable broth to maintain a sauce-like consistency.

Cook the pasta until *al dente*, then drain.

Serve the pasta tossed with the sauce and sprinkled with Parmesan cheese and herbs.

SERVES 4–6

LEFT ◆ *Fettuccine with Broccoli, Spinach, and Carrot Butter*

Pasta with Zucchini, Red Sweet Peppers, and Tomatoes

In this dish spaghetti is tossed with a ratatouille-like vegetable mixture. Sautéing the onions and sweet peppers (capsicums) separately from the other vegetables is important: you are able to taste each vegetable distinctly, rather than having the flavors merging together. The vegetable mixture is even better the day after preparation, so make a double batch — an appetiser the first day and a pasta dish the day after.

2 red sweet peppers (capsicums), cut into strips
1 onion, coarsely chopped
3 tablespoons extra virgin olive oil, or as needed
3 zucchini (courgettes), cut into bite-sized pieces
3 garlic cloves, chopped
salt, to taste
8 oz. (250 g) diced fresh or tinned tomatoes, drained (reserve the juice)
several sprigs of fresh rosemary
½ cup (4 fl. oz., 125 ml) tomato juice
2 tablespoons tomato paste (purée)
12–16 oz. (375–500 g) spaghetti
freshly grated Parmesan cheese, to serve

Sauté the sweet peppers and the onion in a small amount of the oil until they have softened, then place them in an ovenproof earthenware casserole.

In the same pan, sauté the zucchini in several batches, using just a little olive oil. Do not brown them; just let some turn a light golden color. Add the garlic and salt, then place this mixture in the casserole. Add the diced tomatoes and rosemary sprigs.

Put the tomato juice and any juice from the drained tomatoes in the sauté pan. Cook until reduced in volume by about half, then pour over the vegetables.

Bake the vegetable mixture in the oven at 375°F (190°C) for about 30 minutes, then remove. If the mixture is very liquid, pour the juices into a pan, reduce over a high heat, then pour back over the vegetables. Season well with salt and stir in the tomato paste to thicken the mixture.

Cook the pasta until *al dente*, then drain. Toss the pasta with the vegetables, then sprinkle each portion with Parmesan cheese, and serve immediately.

SERVES 4–6

Garlic–Parsley Macaroni with Cauliflower, Zucchini, and Red Sweet Peppers

5 garlic cloves, coarsely chopped
4 tablespoons extra virgin olive oil
2 red sweet peppers (capsicums), cut into strips or diced
½ green sweet pepper (capsicum), cut into strips or diced
2 zucchini (courgettes), sliced
½ head cauliflower, divided into small florets
3 tablespoons tomato paste (purée)
½–¾ cup (4–6 fl. oz., 125–185 ml) water
salt and freshly ground black pepper or cayenne pepper, to taste
handful of fresh parsley, coarsely chopped
12 oz. (375 g) small macaroni

Sauté half the garlic in half the olive oil, then add the red and green sweet peppers and cook together for a few minutes, until they have softened. Remove from the pan.

Sauté the zucchini briefly in the pan, until it is just browned, then remove. Sauté the cauliflower for about 5 minutes or until lightly browned. Return the sweet peppers and zucchini to the pan with the cauliflower, then add the tomato paste and water. Season with salt and black or cayenne pepper, and simmer for 10–15 minutes, or until the vegetables are tender. Add half the parsley and set the mixture aside.

Cook the pasta until *al dente*, then drain.

Heat the remaining garlic in the remaining olive oil until it is a light golden color, then add the drained pasta.

Serve the pasta topped with the vegetable mixture. This is good without cheese, but I sometimes serve it with a fresh vegetable relish, such as beet (beetroot), fennel, diced carrot and tomatoes, tossed in vinaigrette.

SERVES 4

LEFT ♦ *Garlic–Parsley Macaroni with Cauliflower, Zucchini, and Red Sweet Peppers*

Pasta with Provençal Flavors

I once wandered into a café in Arles in Provence and was virtually held captive by the owner, who was fixated, predictably enough, on Van Gogh. His rambling life story was as muddled as the poor artist's, but this artist was of the kitchen rather than the canvas. And in what seemed like a reward for a nearly unendurable afternoon of listening on my part (I was young, my French was not brilliant; I could not figure out how to get up and leave) the café owner served me up portion upon portion of dishes he had invented. They were all related in some obscure way to Van Gogh, and they were all outstandingly delicious. This recipe is my version of the pasta dish he served, redolent with the orange, herb, fennel, and saffron scents of Provence.

1 onion, chopped
1 red sweet pepper (capsicum), diced
3 garlic cloves, chopped
2 tablespoons extra virgin olive oil
½ cup (4 fl. oz., 125 ml) dry white wine
8 ripe tomatoes, chopped, or 14 oz. (435 g) tinned tomatoes, chopped
½ cup (4 fl. oz., 125 ml) tomato juice or tomato purée (passata) (if using fresh tomatoes)
pinch of sugar (optional)
piece of orange rind (zest) 1 in. (25 mm) long
generous pinch of fennel seeds or ½ bulb fresh fennel, coarsely chopped
1 tablespoon tomato paste (purée)
generous pinch of herbes de Provence or other dried mixed herbs
pinch of saffron threads
salt and freshly ground black pepper, to taste
12–16 oz. (375–500 g) pasta such as spaghettini or capellini
finely chopped fresh basil, to serve
Tomato, Beet, and Onion Relish (optional; see below)

Lightly sauté the onion, red sweet pepper, and garlic in the olive oil until they have softened.

Add the white wine and boil until the liquid is reduced in volume by at least half. Add the tomatoes and juice or purée, the sugar (if needed), orange rind, fennel, and tomato paste, and simmer for about 10 minutes, or until full flavored.

Season the sauce with the herbes de Provence or mixed herbs. Toast the saffron in an ungreased skillet (frying pan) until it darkens slightly, then crush it into a powder with the back of a spoon or a mortar and pestle, and add it to the sauce. Season with salt and pepper.

Cook the pasta until *al dente,* then drain. Toss with the sauce, then sprinkle with basil and serve.

VARIATION

Tomato, Beet, and Onion Relish: This tangy, simple-to-prepare relish makes a refreshing addition. Just combine 3 ripe tomatoes (diced) with 2 small cooked beets (beetroot) (diced) and half a chopped onion. Season with 1 garlic clove, chopped, if you like, and dress with olive oil and lemon juice or wine vinegar, to taste.

Couscous Provençal: Prepare the sauce above but double the amount of saffron and add 2 cups (16 fl. oz., 500 ml) of hot vegetable broth (see p. 15). Pour this mixture over 12 oz. (375 g) of instant couscous, dot with a little butter, and cover. Leave for 10 minutes, so the couscous can absorb the liquid, then taste for seasoning. If it is too dry or uncooked, add a little more liquid and heat over a medium flame. Omit the relish.

SERVES 4–6

RIGHT ♦ *Pasta with Provençal Flavors*

Braised Onions

Onions, braised until golden and caramelized as if you were making onion soup or pissaladière, make a delicious basis for simple, gutsy pasta dishes. Since the onions are so tender and sweet, they are best combined with tangy, acidic, or pungent ingredients such as capers, tomatoes, red wine, etc.
Below is the method for braising the onions, followed by two variations. The braised onions make a savory, forceful sauce, and I especially like them on thin strands of spaghettini, though the thicker spaghetti could be used instead.

2 lbs. (1 kg) onions, thinly sliced
2–3 tablespoons extra virgin olive oil

Toss the onions with the olive oil in a heavy pan. Cover, and cook over very low heat, stirring occasionally, for about 30 minutes, or until the onions have softened and turned a light golden color.

Remove the lid and stir, then return the lid and continue to cook for another 30–40 minutes over low to medium heat. Add a little more olive oil, if needed, to keep the onions from sticking. In the end the onions should be meltingly tender, slightly browned and sticky in parts. Use as the basis for the following two recipes.

SERVES 4–6

Pasta with Pissaladière-style Sauce of Onions and Olives

Braised onions and salty black olives make an intriguing plateful: the combination is traditional for the Niçoise flat bread pissaladière, and while it may be a surprise served on pasta, it is hearty and delicious.

1 lb. (500 g) spaghettini
braised onions (see above)
20–30 black olives (kalamata, Greek, Niçoise, or oil-cured), pitted and cut into quarters
marjoram, thyme or other herbs, either fresh or dried, to taste
salt and freshly ground black pepper, to taste
freshly grated Parmesan cheese, to serve

Cook the spaghettini until *al dente*.

Meanwhile, heat the braised onions over medium-high heat. Remove from the heat and add the olives, herbs, salt (if needed — the olives are salty) and the pepper.

Drain the pasta and toss it with the onion sauce, then serve immediately, sprinkled generously with cheese.

SERVES 4–6

Spaghettini with Provençal Onion Sauce, Seasoned with Capers and Tomatoes

3 garlic cloves, chopped
2 tablespoons extra virgin olive oil
12 ripe tomatoes, peeled, seeded and diced, or 1½ tins (14 oz., 435 g tins) chopped tomatoes
braised onions (see above)
large pinch of dried thyme
pinch of sugar
salt and freshly ground black pepper, to taste
2 tablespoons capers
1 lb. (500 g) spaghettini
freshly grated Parmesan or other hard grating cheese, to serve

Heat the garlic in the olive oil and when it is fragrant but not browned, add the tomatoes. Stir them through until they are perfumed and heated, then remove the dish from the heat. Stir through the braised onions. Season with the thyme, sugar, salt and pepper, and capers. Set aside and keep warm.

Meanwhile, cook the spaghettini until *al dente*, then drain. Toss the pasta with the sauce. Serve immediately, sprinkled generously with cheese.

SERVES 4–6

Fettuccine or Tagliatelle with Creamy Onion Sauce

This sauce of sautéed onions and garlic awash with nutmeg-scented cream is as delicious as it is unusual. A generous sprinkling of crunchy toasted breadcrumbs makes the dish outstanding.
Since it is fairly rich, serve as a first course or a side dish.

2 oz. (60 g) stale French or Italian-style bread
2 tablespoons vegetable oil or 1 oz. (30 g) butter, for frying breadcrumbs
salt and freshly ground black pepper, to taste
6 onions, coarsely chopped
3 garlic cloves, coarsely chopped
1½ oz. (45 g) butter
2½ cups (1 imp. pint, 625 ml) light (single) cream
pinch of freshly grated nutmeg
1 lb. (500 g) fettuccine or tagliatelle
freshly grated Parmesan cheese, to serve

Grate the bread on the large holes of a grater to make crumbs. Toast the crumbs in the vegetable oil or butter in a heavy skillet (frying pan) over a medium heat until they are golden brown. Remove from the heat, season with salt and pepper, and set aside.

Sauté the onion and garlic in the remaining butter until they are lightly browned. Stir in the cream, cook for a minute or two, then season with the nutmeg and salt and pepper. Set aside.

Meanwhile, cook the pasta until *al dente*, then drain.

Toss the pasta in the sauce, then sprinkle generously with the toasted breadcrumbs and Parmesan cheese, and serve.

SERVES 6

ABOVE ♦ *Pasta with Pissaladière-style Sauce of Onions and Chives*

Farfalle with Pumpkin and Mild Red Chili Pepper

The spicy flavors of America's Southwest — garlic, pumpkin, tomatoes, and mild red chili pepper — season this pasta. It is informal, dryish rather than saucy, and very easily put together. For health reasons the dish may be made with extra virgin olive oil, and it is good, but I must confess that I often use butter: the taste of butter-sautéed garlic, pumpkin and red chili pepper is utterly seductive.
Any sort of chunky or flat pasta may be used instead of the farfalle.

8 oz. (250 g) pumpkin, peeled and diced
1½ oz. (45 g) butter
5–8 garlic cloves, coarsely chopped
5–8 fresh or well-drained tinned tomatoes, diced
2 teaspoons mild red chili pepper powder
1 teaspoon paprika
¼ teaspoon cumin, or to taste
1 lb. (500 g) pasta of choice
salt, to taste
2 oz. (60 g) freshly grated Parmesan cheese,
    to serve

Lightly sauté the pumpkin in half the butter for several minutes, until it just becomes tender, then add the garlic and cook for another moment or two.

Stir in the tomatoes and cook them through, then sprinkle in the chili pepper powder, paprika, and cumin. Cook a minute or two longer, then remove from the heat.

Meanwhile, cook the pasta until *al dente*, then drain.

Toss the pasta with the remaining butter and the sauce. Season with salt to taste, then toss with the Parmesan cheese. Serve immediately.

SERVES 4–6

Fettuccine with Creamy Pumpkin and Red Sweet Pepper Sauce

This golden-hued sauce is suave and creamy, with sweet, earthy pumpkin (or other winter squash) and fresh red sweet peppers (capsicums), enlivened with a flurry of pungent Parmesan cheese. It is a delicate and memorable dish, best served as a rich first course rather than a main plateful.

1 onion, chopped
1 garlic clove, chopped
1½ oz. (45 g) butter
1 lb. (500 g) pumpkin (or other winter squash),
    peeled and diced
½ red sweet pepper (capsicum), diced
½ bouillon (stock) cube
1 cup (8 fl. oz., 250 ml) water
1¼ cups (10 fl. oz., 310 ml) light (single) cream
large pinch of dried thyme
freshly ground black pepper and cayenne pepper,
    to taste
12 oz. (375 g) dried fettuccine or 1 lb. (500 g)
    fresh fettuccine
freshly grated Parmesan cheese, to serve

Lightly sauté the onion and garlic in two-thirds of the butter until they have just softened, then add the pumpkin and sauté until it is lightly browned and almost tender. Add the red sweet pepper and continue cooking for a few minutes, until the pumpkin and sweet peppers have softened.

Add the bouillon cube and water, increase the heat, and cook until the liquid is reduced by about three-quarters. The pumpkin should be cooked through.

Add the cream, heat through, and season with the thyme, pepper, and cayenne pepper. Keep this mixture warm while you cook the pasta. (The sauce may be made in advance, then reheated with a little water when ready to serve.)

When the pasta is *al dente*, drain it. Toss the pasta with the sauce, top each portion with a good dusting of Parmesan cheese, then serve immediately.

SERVES 4

LEFT ♦ *Farfalle with Pumpkin and Mild Red Chili Pepper*

Gnocchi with Artichoke, Porcini, and Carrot

While gnocchi usually refers to soft dumplings made from potatoes, it is also the name of a particularly chewy shell-shaped pasta, which is good with rich vegetable sauces such as this one. Here, the rich sauce is tempered by a grating of fresh carrot.

½ oz. (15 g) dried porcini mushrooms
2 cups (16 fl. oz., 500 ml) hot, but not quite
    boiling, water
1 onion, finely chopped
3 garlic cloves, chopped
2 tablespoons extra virgin olive oil
3 fresh artichoke hearts (prepared as on p. 18),
    cut into large dice, or 8 drained (if tinned) or
    thawed (if frozen) artichoke hearts
1 carrot, coarsely grated
3 fl. oz. (90 ml) light (single) cream
salt and freshly ground black pepper, to taste
small squeeze of lemon juice (unless using tinned
    artichokes; they are acidic enough)
12–16 oz. (375–500 g) dried shell-shaped pasta
    gnocchi or other seashell pasta
1–2 oz. (30–60 g) butter
freshly grated Parmesan cheese, to serve

Rehydrate the mushrooms in the hot water (see p. 17), reserving the liquid. Set aside.

Sauté the onion and garlic in the olive oil until softened, then mix in the artichoke hearts. Add the porcini and grated carrot and cook through for 3–4 minutes.

Pour the reserved mushroom soaking liquid into the pan and cook until reduced by about half. Swirl the cream through, and season with salt and pepper, and a dash of lemon juice. Set aside.

Cook the pasta until *al dente,* then drain. Toss the pasta with the butter, and serve with the sauce, offering Parmesan cheese separately.

SERVES 4–6

Fettuccine with Creamy Diced Artichoke Sauce

Rich and elegant, this is very quick and easy to make once the artichokes have been prepared and blanched. It really does need to be made with fresh artichokes to avoid the acidic flavors that often develop in tinned or frozen ones. Almost any pasta shape can be used — spaghetti, penne, pappardelle — but the delicacy of good-quality fresh fettuccine makes this dish special.

4–5 medium to large artichokes (prepared
    as on p. 18)
1 small onion, chopped
1 garlic clove, chopped
1 oz. (30 g) butter
½ cup (4 fl. oz., 125 ml) vegetable broth (see p. 15)
1¼ cups (10 fl. oz., 310 ml) light (single) cream
pinch of cayenne pepper or freshly ground
    black pepper
1 lb. (500 g) fresh fettuccine or 12 oz. (375 g)
    dried fettuccine
freshly grated Parmesan cheese, to serve

Dice the blanched artichokes, then set aside.

Lightly sauté the onion and garlic in the butter. When softened, add the artichokes and cook together for a few minutes.

Add the broth. Bring the sauce to the boil, then let it simmer for 5–8 minutes, until the artichokes are quite tender. Add the cream, heat the sauce through, and season with cayenne or black pepper. Salt is unlikely to be needed as both the broth and the Parmesan cheese are salty. Cover and set aside while you cook the pasta.

Cook the pasta until just tender. Drain and toss with the sauce, then serve immediately, sprinkled with Parmesan cheese.

SERVES 4

RIGHT ♦ *Gnocchi with Artichoke, Porcini, and Carrot*

Pasta with Green Beans, Red Sweet Peppers, Olives, Basil, and Pine Nuts

A gaily colored dish with fresh and lively flavors. The amounts given need not be followed exactly.

2 red sweet peppers (capsicums), diced
6 garlic cloves, chopped
3 tablespoons extra virgin olive oil
salt and freshly ground black pepper, to taste
1 lb. (500 g) spaghetti
8 oz. (250 g) green or string beans, cut into
   bite-sized lengths
3 tablespoons toasted pine nuts
about 15 black olives (kalamata, oil-cured),
   pitted and quartered
about 10 fresh basil leaves, thinly sliced

Sauté the sweet peppers and half the garlic in the olive oil until they have just softened and are lightly browned in places. Season with salt and pepper. Set aside and keep warm.

Cook the spaghetti until half-done, then add the beans and continue cooking until both the beans and pasta are *al dente*; drain.

Toss the spaghetti and beans with the sautéed sweet peppers and garlic, the remaining garlic, the pine nuts, olives, and basil. Serve immediately or at room temperature (warm).

VARIATION
Substitute 4 diced and well-drained tomatoes for the sweet peppers.

SERVES 4–6

Pasta with a Sauce of Spinach, Peas, and Rosemary Cream

Hearty and thick, filled with a garden full of vegetables and a splash of cream. While I never throw away the liquid from cooking vegetables, sometimes I am at a loss as to what to do with it. Here the decision is made for the cook, with a sauce conveniently based on the vegetable cooking water mixed with a bouillon (stock) cube.

1 lb. (500 g) fresh spinach or 12 oz. (375 g)
    frozen spinach
½ bouillon (stock) cube
1 onion, chopped
5 garlic cloves, chopped
1½ oz. (45 g) butter
1 tablespoon extra virgin olive oil
1 tablespoon chopped fresh rosemary, or to taste
4–6 oz. (125–185 g) fresh or frozen peas
1 lb. (500 g) penne, or other short, chubby shapes
    such as lumache (shells), etc.
3 zucchini (courgettes), cut into large dice
1 cup (8 fl. oz., 250 ml) light (single) cream
2 teaspoons lemon juice, or to taste
salt and freshly ground black pepper, to taste
fresh herbs such as basil, rosemary or parsley,
    to serve (optional)
freshly grated Parmesan cheese, to serve

Cook the spinach in ½ cup (4 fl. oz, 125 ml) of water, until the spinach is bright green. Remove the spinach from the cooking liquid (reserving the liquid for use in the sauce), rinse with cold water, and drain. When cool enough to handle, squeeze the spinach until nearly dry, reserving the green liquid that results. Add this and the bouillon cube to the cooking liquid and set aside for the sauce.

Lightly sauté the onion and garlic in the butter and olive oil until just softened; stir in 1 cup (8 fl. oz., 250 ml) of the spinach cooking liquid and cook until the liquid is reduced to about a quarter of its original volume.

Add the reserved spinach, the rosemary and peas, and cook for a 3–4 minutes until heated through, adding a little more of the spinach cooking water if the mixture is in danger of burning. The mixture should be nearly dry, not soupy. Set aside and keep warm.

Cook the pasta and zucchini until *al dente*, then drain. Stir the pasta and zucchini into the spinach and pea mixture, then add the cream and lemon juice. Season with salt and pepper, and herbs, then serve immediately. Top each portion with a sprinkling of Parmesan cheese.

VARIATION

This hearty vegetable and pasta dish makes a good casserole: pour it into an earthenware casserole, top with a layer of fontina or Asiago cheese and a sprinkling of Parmesan, then bake in the oven at 375°F (190°C) until the top is lightly browned in parts. Serve immediately.

SERVES 4–6

Pasta with Basil-scented Walnut Pesto

This is a Tuscan pesto-like sauce of pounded nuts and basil. You can vary the amounts of basil and walnuts to taste and the garlic is optional but not traditional. Another version of the sauce, Ravioli con Salsa di Noci (see p. 68), includes mascarpone, which makes it richer and smoother, a classic to slather over Genoese pansotti (ravioli stuffed with spinach and ricotta).

several large handfuls of fresh basil, about
    50 leaves, coarsely chopped
7 oz. (225 g) shelled walnuts, coarsely chopped
salt and freshly ground black pepper or cayenne
    pepper, to taste
2 oz. (60 g) Parmesan cheese, freshly grated,
    plus extra, to serve
¾ cup (6 fl. oz., 185 ml) extra virgin olive oil
12 oz. (375 g) pasta of choice

Grind the basil together with the walnuts. This can be done in a blender (liquidizer) or food processor.

Season with salt and pepper or cayenne pepper. Add the Parmesan cheese and olive oil, and mix to a creamy consistency.

Cook the pasta until *al dente*, then drain and toss with the sauce. Serve with extra Parmesan cheese.

SERVES 4

Spaghetti with Hazelnut Pesto

This rich yet savory hazelnut paste is very similar to pesto, but with a strong taste of pounded nuts rather than the herbal flavor of basil. The similarity between the two sauces should be no surprise, since both hail from Liguria, and hazelnuts are enjoyed in nearly as many dishes there as is basil.

In season the nuts are sold from impromptu street stalls, threaded onto strings like chunky necklaces. While their destination is usually sweets and baked goods, here they star in a deliciously unusual pasta, a satisfying dish for autumn or winter.

3–4 oz. (90–125 g) shelled hazelnuts
4–5 garlic cloves, chopped
about ¼ cup (2 fl. oz., 60 ml) extra virgin olive oil
12 oz. (375 g) spaghetti
1 tablespoon fresh thyme leaves or ¼–½ teaspoon
    dried thyme
freshly ground black pepper to taste
1 oz. (30 g) Parmesan cheese, freshly grated,
    or to taste
1 oz. (30 g) fresh parsley, chopped, or to taste

Toast the hazelnuts in an ungreased heavy skillet (frying pan) over medium to high heat, tossing them frequently to prevent burning. They should become flecked with dark brown. When they are nearly ready their skins will split and begin to fall off. (Hazelnuts may also be roasted in the oven at 400°F (200°C) for about 10 minutes.) Place the hazelnuts in a clean towel and rub them against each other briskly to remove their skins.

In a blender (liquidizer) or food processor, finely chop the garlic then add the hazelnuts and process to a coarse mealy texture. Add enough olive oil to make a thinnish paste, then set aside.

Cook the pasta until *al dente*, then drain. Toss the pasta with the hazelnut paste and the thyme, and season with the pepper. Add a little more olive oil if the paste is too thick.

Serve immediately, seasoned with black pepper and sprinkled with the Parmesan cheese and parsley.

SERVES 4

Pasta with Creamy Sauce of Puréed Mushrooms and Porcini

This sauce is based on a combination of cultivated mushrooms and the more flavorful porcini, simmered with cream, then puréed into a rich mushroom essence.

½ oz. (15 g) dried porcini
1 cup (8 fl. oz., 250 ml) hot, but not boiling,
    vegetable broth (see p. 15) or water
1 onion, chopped
2 tablespoons extra virgin olive oil
8 oz. (250 g) mushrooms, coarsely chopped
3 garlic cloves, chopped
several gratings of fresh nutmeg
½ cup (4 fl. oz., 125 ml) light (single) cream
salt and freshly ground black pepper, to taste
1 lb. (500 g) fresh pasta such as fettuccine
½ oz. (15 g) butter
freshly grated Parmesan cheese, to serve

Rehydrate the porcini in the broth or water (see p. 17), reserving the liquid.

Sauté the onion in the olive oil until it is softened and lightly browned in places, then add the fresh mushrooms and the garlic. Cook until the mushrooms are browned and reduced in size.

Add the porcini to the mushrooms, then add several tablespoons of the soaking liquid and cook until the liquid has evaporated. Remove from the heat and add the nutmeg.

In a blender (liquidizer) or food processor, blend the mushroom mixture with the cream and ½ cup (4 fl. oz., 125 ml) of the soaking liquid until smooth. Season with salt and pepper. Keep warm.

Cook the pasta until *al dente*, then drain. Toss the pasta in the butter. Toss with the sauce and serve immediately. Offer Parmesan cheese separately.

SERVES 4–6

Capellini with Peas, Porcini, and Tomatoes

Porcini mushrooms scent the zesty tomatoes and bright green peas in this flavorsome pasta dish.
The amount of porcini you use will, of course, affect the flavor of the sauce, but it is equally good if you add only a few. Finishing the dish with a little nugget of melting butter and a scattering of snipped basil gives it an even richer flavor.

1 oz. (30 g) dried porcini
¾ cup (6 fl. oz., 185 ml) very hot, but not boiling, vegetable broth (see p. 15) or water
1 small onion, coarsely chopped
2 garlic cloves, chopped
1½ oz. (45 g) butter
8 ripe tomatoes, diced, or 14 oz. (435 g) tinned tomatoes, drained and diced
1 tablespoon tomato paste (purée)
salt and freshly ground black pepper, to taste
tiny pinch of sugar (optional)
12 oz. (375 g) capellini
4 oz. (125 g) fresh young peas or frozen petits pois
5–8 fresh basil leaves, thinly sliced
freshly grated Parmesan or similar hard grating cheese, to serve

Rehydrate the porcini in the broth or water (see p. 17), reserving the liquid.

Lightly sauté the onion and garlic in two-thirds of the butter until they have softened. Add the porcini and cook for only a moment. Add the reserved soaking liquid, bring to the boil and cook until the liquid is reduced to less than half its volume.

Add the tomatoes and cook for a minute or two longer, then add the tomato paste and season with salt, pepper, and the sugar (if using).

Meanwhile, cook the pasta and peas together in boiling water, then drain. Toss with the sauce, then with the remaining butter. Serve immediately, sprinkled with the basil. Offer Parmesan cheese separately.

SERVES 4

RIGHT ♦ *Capellini with Peas, Porcini, and Tomatoes*

Capellini or Fettuccine with Asparagus and a Creamy Purée of Hazelnuts, Porcini, and Mascarpone Cheese

The subtle flavors of hazelnuts, porcini, and mascarpone cheese make a luscious sauce, especially when served with delicate pasta and asparagus. If asparagus is out of season, don't worry, the dish is delicious without it. There is no Parmesan cheese here; I like the strong flavors of this sauce to shine through rather than be blanketed by the cheese.

1 oz. (30 g) dried porcini
¾–1 cup (6–8 fl. oz., 185–250 ml) hot, but not boiling, vegetable broth (see p. 15)
2 oz. (60 g) hazelnuts
2 garlic cloves, chopped
6–8 oz. (185–250 g) mascarpone cheese
¼ cup (2 fl. oz., 60 ml) Marsala or brandy (optional)
salt and freshly ground black pepper, to taste
12 oz. (375 g) capellini or fettuccine, preferably fresh
8–12 oz. (250–375 g) asparagus, tough ends trimmed, cut into bite-sized pieces
½–1 oz. (15–30 g) butter (optional)

Rehydrate the porcini in the broth (see p. 17), reserving the liquid. Lightly toast the hazelnuts in an ungreased heavy skillet (frying pan) until they are lightly browned. Remove from the pan, place in a clean towel and rub the nuts against each other to remove the skins; leave to cool.

In a blender (liquidizer) or food processor, finely chop the garlic, then add the toasted hazelnuts and process until some are finely ground, others quite chunky. Add the rehydrated porcini, the soaking liquid and the mascarpone cheese, then process together. (This may be done up to a day ahead and kept refrigerated.)

Add the Marsala or brandy; cook over medium to high heat until the liquid is reduced by half and intensified in color and flavor. Season with salt and pepper.

Cook the pasta and the asparagus together in boiling water. If using fresh pasta, add the asparagus at the beginning; if using dried pasta, add the asparagus after about 4 minutes; drain.

Toss the hot pasta and asparagus in the butter (if using), then with the rich sauce, and serve.

SERVES 4

Pasta with Grilled Summer Vegetables, Northern California Style

Vegetables on the grill are as much a part of Californian eating and cooking as garlic, olive oil, and local wines. One of the delightful things about grilled vegetables is the way their smoky flavor enhances other dishes such as soups, pizza, sandwiches, or the following pasta dish.

2–3 zucchini (courgettes), and/or other summer squash, cut lengthwise into thin slices
1 red, 1 yellow and 1 green sweet pepper (caspicum)
1 Japanese-style eggplant (aubergine), sliced lengthwise
bunch of scallions (spring onions), trimmed but left whole
1 bulb fresh fennel, cut lengthwise into thin slices
½ cup (4 fl. oz., 125 ml) extra virgin olive oil
juice of ½–1 lemon
6 garlic cloves, finely chopped
dried thyme or herbes de Provence, to taste
6 ripe tomatoes
1 lb. (500 g) fresh or 12 oz. (375 g) dried pasta of choice
8 oil-marinated sun-dried tomatoes, sliced thinly
salt and freshly ground black pepper, to taste
handful of mixed fresh herbs: basil, oregano, parsley, thyme, etc.

Place the zucchini, sweet peppers, eggplant, scallions, and fennel in a baking dish and pour over the olive oil and lemon juice. Sprinkle over half the garlic and the dried herbs and leave for at least an hour.

Remove the vegetables from the dish and reserve the marinade. Grill the marinated vegetables and the whole tomatoes over an open fire (or under a hot grill (broiler), though this will not have the lovely smoky aroma) until tender but still quite firm. Remove from the grill. Peel and dice the tomatoes, and slice the other vegetables into matchsticks. Keep the vegetables warm.

Cook the pasta until *al dente,* then drain.

Toss with the reserved marinade, the remaining garlic, sun-dried tomatoes, and grilled vegetables. Season with salt and pepper and serve strewn with lots of fresh herbs.

SERVES 6

Rigatoni with White Beans, Tomato–Parsley Sauce, and Red Pesto

4–5 garlic cloves, chopped
2 tablespoons extra virgin olive oil
½ oz. (15 g) parsley, coarsely chopped
14 oz. (435 g) cooked or drained tinned white kidney beans, or cannellini beans
1 lb. (500 g) ripe tomatoes, diced, or 14 oz. (435 g) tinned tomatoes, chopped
pinch of sugar (optional)
salt and freshly ground black pepper, to taste
1 lb. (500 g) rigatoni or other short thick pasta
6 oz. (185 g) red pesto (see p. 16)
2–3 tablespoons coarsely chopped fresh basil, to serve (optional)
freshly grated Parmesan cheese, to serve

Heat the garlic in the olive oil until it is fragrant but not browned, then stir in the parsley and beans and cook for a few moments.

Add the tomatoes and cook over medium to high heat for a minute or two, until most of the liquid evaporates. Season with sugar (if using), and salt and pepper. Set aside and keep warm.

Cook the pasta until *al dente,* then drain.

Toss the pasta with the sauce and red pesto. Serve sprinkled with fresh basil (if using), and Parmesan cheese.

VARIATION
Instead of white kidney beans or cannellini beans, use cooked or drained tinned butter beans (large dried white lima beans). To the sautéing garlic add 1 diced red sweet pepper (capsicum), then proceed as above.

SERVES 4–6

LEFT ♦ *Pasta with Grilled Summer Vegetables, Northern California Style*

Spaghettini with Diced Roasted Tomatoes and Pungent Raw Garlic

Once you have the tomatoes roasted, the rest of this dish is a cinch. I find that roasting the tomatoes the day before is not only easier, but the tomatoes taste better and their juices have thickened nicely.

20 smallish ripe, red tomatoes
5 garlic cloves, coarsely chopped
3 tablespoons extra virgin olive oil
salt and freshly ground black pepper, to taste

1 lb. (500 g) spaghettini
½–1 oz. (15–30 g) butter (optional)

Roast the tomatoes (see p. 18).

Combine the chopped roasted tomatoes and their juices with the garlic and the olive oil. Season with salt and pepper.

Cook the pasta until *al dente*, then drain. Toss the pasta in the butter (if using), then with the tomato mixture, and serve immediately.

SERVES 4–6

Ditalini with Fennel-scented Peas

This very light sauce is based on peas in a reduction of onion- and garlic-scented broth, flavored with fennel seed. Leftovers are delicious spooned into a light tomato or mushroom broth, vegetable soup, or minestrone.

2 onions, chopped
4 garlic cloves, chopped
1 oz. (30 g) butter or 2 tablespoons extra virgin olive oil, or a mixture of the two
2 tablespoons chopped fresh parsley
8 oz. (250 g) fresh or frozen peas
2 cups (16 fl. oz., 500 ml) vegetable broth (see p. 15)
large pinch each of mixed dried herbs and fennel seeds
12 oz. (375 g) ditalini, elbows, or other short pasta
salt and freshly ground black pepper, to taste
freshly grated Parmesan cheese, to serve

Lightly sauté the onions and garlic in the butter and/or olive oil until they have just softened.

Add the parsley and peas and cook for a minute or two, until both are bright green, then add the broth. Cook over a very high heat until the liquid is reduced to only a few tablespoons and has a very intense flavor.

Add the herbs and fennel seeds and the sauce aside.

Meanwhile, cook the pasta until *al dente,* then drain. Toss the pasta with the pea sauce, season with salt and pepper, then serve, sprinkled generously with Parmesan cheese.

VARIATION

Tomato Broth with Peas and Ditalini: Prepare this fragrant soup with any leftover peas and ditalini you have. Sauté several garlic cloves (chopped) in 1 tablespoon of extra virgin olive oil, then stir in 6–8 diced, ripe tomatoes (1 cup) and 4 cups (1¾ imp. pints, 1 litre) of vegetable broth (see p. 15). Bring to the boil, then add the leftover peas and ditalini and heat through. Season with salt, pepper, and herbs, and sprinkle with freshly grated Parmesan or pecorino cheese.

SERVES 4

LEFT ♦ *Ditalini with Fennel-scented Peas*

Spaghetti with Lusty Tomato and Pea Sauce

Peas seasoned with fennel and Italian herbs such as thyme or marjoram make a robust tomato sauce that is good with nearly any hearty pasta, such as penne, spaghetti, fusilli lunghi, etc. I often grate very unItalian cheeses over this — Cheddar, Monterey Jack, or Cantal — and they are delicious.

1 small onion, chopped
3 garlic cloves, chopped
2 tablespoons extra virgin olive oil
2 lbs. (1 kg) ripe tomatoes, chopped, or 1½ tins (14 oz., 435 g tins) tomatoes, chopped
2 tablespoons tomato paste (purée) (optional)
pinch of sugar
12 oz. (375 g) fresh or frozen peas
½ teaspoon dried mixed herbs or thyme, or to taste
¼ teaspoon fennel seeds, or to taste
salt and freshly ground black pepper, to taste
12–16 oz. (375–500 g) spaghetti
handful of chopped fresh parsley or basil
freshly grated Parmesan or other sharp grating cheese, to serve

Lightly sauté the onion and garlic in the olive oil. When soft and translucent, add the tomatoes, crushing them as you add them, tomato paste, sugar, peas, dried herbs, and fennel seeds. Bring to the boil and cook over medium to high heat for about 10 minutes, or until the peas are tender and the tomato sauce has thickened. Season with salt and pepper.

Meanwhile, cook the pasta until *al dente;* drain. Toss the pasta with the sauce. Serve immediately, sprinkled with parsley or basil and the cheese.

VARIATIONS

Tricolor Spaghetti with Tomato and Pea Sauce: Serve the sauce ladled over tricolor spaghetti. The robust sauce is particularly good with the hearty quality of the multi-vegetable pasta.

Macaroni with Peas and Ricotta: Serve the sauce with short, fat macaroni shapes, and top each portion with a dollop of creamy ricotta and a flurry of coarsely grated Parmesan cheese.

SERVES 4–6

Tiny Seashells or Orzo with Radicchio

Radicchio, with its slightly bitter and invigorating flavor, pairs pleasingly with this wine, tomato, and cream sauce. If radicchio is unavailable, use a different bitter salad leaf, such as chicory (Belgian endive) or Treviso.

1 onion, chopped
3 garlic cloves, coarsely chopped
3 tablespoons extra virgin olive oil
2–3 heads radicchio, trimmed and coarsely chopped
1 cup (8 fl. oz., 250 ml) dry red wine
4 ripe fresh or tinned tomatoes, peeled and diced
1 cup (8 fl. oz., 250 ml) light (single) cream
1 lb. (500 g) small seashell-shaped pasta or orzo
freshly grated Parmesan cheese or crumbled
   Gorgonzola cheese, to serve
handful of fresh basil, chopped or thinly sliced
   (use parsley if basil is unavailable)

Lightly sauté the onion and garlic in the olive oil until they have softened, then stir the radicchio through.

Pour in the wine and cook over medium to high heat until the liquid is reduced by about half. Add the tomatoes and cream and simmer until the liquid becomes a thinnish sauce.

Meanwhile, cook the pasta until *al dente*, then drain. Toss the pasta with the radicchio sauce, then sprinkle with the Parmesan or Gorgonzola cheese and the basil or parsley, and serve.

SERVES 4

Ditalini and Broccoli with Creamy Blue Cheese Sauce

While combining blue cheese such as Gorgonzola with pasta is a delicious Italian tradition, adding richness and smoothness to the sauce, the pungency of the blue-veined cheese does mellow and lose its characteristic bite as it heats. Here, half the blue cheese is added at the beginning, for richness, and half at the end, for a tangy jolt.

½ oz. (15 g) butter
1 tablespoon flour
1 cup (8 fl. oz., 250 ml) milk
8 oz. (250 g) blue cheese, crumbled
salt and freshly ground black pepper, to taste
tiny pinch of cayenne pepper
12 oz. (375 g) ditalini or similar pasta
1–2 bunches broccoli, cut into bite-sized florets

Melt the butter in a pan, then sprinkle in the flour. Cook for a few minutes, until the flour is golden, then remove from the heat. Stir in a little of the milk to make a smooth paste, then gradually add the rest. Return to the heat and cook, stirring, until thickened. Remove from the heat again and stir in half the blue cheese. Season with the salt and pepper, and the cayenne pepper.

Cook the pasta until half done. Add the broccoli and continue cooking until both broccoli and pasta are *al dente*, then drain.

Toss the broccoli and pasta with the sauce, then crumble the remaining blue cheese over, toss well, and serve immediately.

SERVES 4

RIGHT ♦ *Tiny Seashells or Orzo with Radicchio*

Fusilli with Diced Autumn Vegetables

A selection of coarsely chopped vegetables, combined with the strong flavor of porcini, makes an unusual sauce. Toss with supple chewy fusilli — the kind that curls around rather than twists. If it is unavailable, capellini would be nice.

½ oz. (15 g) dried porcini
4 oz. (125 g) mushrooms, coarsely chopped
3 tablespoons extra virgin olive oil
2 onions, coarsely chopped
3 garlic cloves, coarsely chopped
salt and freshly ground black pepper, to taste
½ carrot, coarsely chopped
½ zucchini (courgette), coarsely chopped
4 fresh or tinned artichoke hearts, cut into coarse
    dice (prepare as on p. 18)
2 ripe tomatoes or 3 tinned ones, diced
12–16 oz. (375–500 g) fusilli or capellini
½ oz. (15 g) butter
freshly grated Parmesan cheese, to serve

Rehydrate the porcini (see p. 17). Coarsely chop the porcini and set aside.

Sauté the fresh mushrooms in half the oil with half the onions until the mushrooms and onions are lightly browned in places and richly flavored. Add the rehydrated porcini and half the garlic, then season with salt and pepper. Remove the mixture from the pan and set aside.

In the same pan, using the remainder of the olive oil, sauté the remaining onion and garlic, plus the carrot and zucchini. When the vegetables are softened, add the artichoke hearts and sauté for a moment or two. Add the tomatoes, then cook over medium to high heat until the mixture becomes slightly sauce-like.

Cook the pasta until *al dente*, then drain. Toss the pasta with the butter first, then with the vegetable mixture. Serve sprinkled with Parmesan cheese.

VARIATION

Autumn Vegetable Ragu: Purée the vegetable mixture with 1 cup (8 fl. oz., 250 ml) of the mushroom soaking liquid and 2 small tins (6–8 tablespoons) of tomato paste. Season with a drop or two of lemon juice, salt and pepper, and several large pinches of mixed herbs. This mixture also makes a delicious pizza topping: smear a tablespoon or so of tomato paste on top of the pizza (dough) base, then top with several spoonfuls of the vegetable sauce. Sprinkle with olive oil, raw garlic and finely grated cheese, then bake until lightly browned. Serve topped with several spoonfuls of chopped raw tomatoes and a generous sprinkling of mixed herbs such as herbes de Provence.

SERVES 4–6

Autumn Day Capellini with Roasted Garlic, Mushrooms, and Tomatoes

2 heads garlic, separated into cloves, unpeeled,
4 garlic cloves, peeled and chopped
4 tablespoons extra virgin olive oil
8 oz. (250 g) mushrooms, thinly sliced
about 15 ripe sweet tomatoes, seeded and diced,
    drained of excess liquid (save for soup or sauce)
salt and freshly ground black pepper, to taste
1 lb. (500 g) capellini
freshly grated pecorino or similar hard grating
    cheese, to serve (optional)
fresh herbs such as parsley, oregano, thyme,
    marjoram, etc., or pinch of thyme or
    herbes de Provence, to serve

Place the whole garlic cloves in a baking dish and toss with a small amount of the olive oil. Bake in the oven at 350°F (180°C) for about 30 minutes, or until the garlic is tender. Leave to cool, then peel the garlic cloves, keeping them from falling apart into a purée as much as you can. Set aside.

Over a high heat, sauté the sliced mushrooms with half the chopped raw garlic in a tablespoon or so of the olive oil, then add the tomatoes and sauté together for a minute or two. Season with salt and pepper and set aside.

Cook the capellini until *al dente*, then drain and toss with the remaining olive oil and chopped raw garlic.

Toss the garlicky pasta with the reserved roasted garlic and the mushroom and tomato mixture. Serve immediately, sprinkled with cheese (if using), and fresh or dried herbs.

SERVES 4–6

LEFT ◆ *Fusilli with Diced Autumn Vegetables*

Penne or Gnocchetti with a Pesto of Mushrooms and Black Olives

Mushrooms and olives cooked into a paste are used to cloak al dente pasta. It tastes outstanding, with the woodsy scent and flavor of the forest.

Penne, gnocchetti, and chunky pastas are a good choice: not only are they sturdy but the little hollows and folds trap bits of the savory mushroom and olive paste. However, flat, narrow pastas such as vermicelli or tagliarini are also quite good.

12 oz. (375 g) mushrooms, coarsely shredded
2–3 garlic cloves, chopped
3–4 tablespoons extra virgin olive oil, plus extra for tossing the pasta

4 oz. (125 g) black olive paste or black olives (kalamata, oil-cured), pitted and finely chopped
12–16 oz. (375–500 g) penne, gnocchetti, or other chunky pasta
1 ½ teaspoons chopped fresh rosemary, or to taste
large pinch of dried mixed herbs
freshly ground black pepper, to taste

Sauté the mushrooms and garlic in the olive oil until the mushrooms are cooked through and the mixture is quite paste-like. Add the olive paste (or olives) and set aside.

Cook the pasta until *al dente*, then drain.

Toss the pasta with a little olive oil and the rosemary, mixed herbs, pepper, and reserved mushroom and olive mixture. Serve immediately.

SERVES 4–6

Couscous Pilaf with Shiitake

Shiitake mushrooms (Chinese black mushrooms) give this wonderful woodsy couscous a European flavor. You could use fresh shiitake, or any of the more unusual mushrooms, but dried ones have a more concentrated flavor, along with the bonus of their soaking liquid.
This makes a cozy supper served with a salad of continental leaves such as frisée (curly endive), arugula (rocket), chives, etc., and perhaps a nice chunk of cheese and plate of ripe nectarines or pears to end the meal.

10–15 dried shiitake (Chinese black mushrooms)
3¼ cps (1½ imp. pints, 800 ml) hot, but not boiling, vegetable broth (see p. 15)
12 oz. (375 g) instant couscous
1 onion, coarsely chopped
3 garlic cloves, coarsely chopped
1½ oz. (45 g) butter
several large pinches of thyme or dried mixed herbs, such as herbes de Provence
light grating of fresh nutmeg
salt and freshly ground black pepper, to taste

Rehydrate the shiitake in the broth (see p. 17), reserving the soaking liquid. Cut off the stems and discard. Slice the caps and set aside.

Moisten the couscous with ⅓–½ cup (3–4 fl. oz., 90–125 ml) cold water, mix well, and set aside.

Sauté the onion and garlic in two-thirds of the butter until softened, then add the shiitake and cook for 5–7 minutes, until the mixture is golden and lightly browned in places. Season with the thyme or mixed herbs, nutmeg, salt, and pepper.

Pour the reserved soaking liquid into the pan and bring to the boil. Continue to boil for a minute or two, then pour into the couscous and mix well. Cover and leave for 5 minutes, or long enough for the couscous to plump up.

Serve immediately, dotted with the remaining butter, which will melt in.

S E R V E S   4 – 6

Spaghetti with Curried Broccoli and Chickpeas

1 onion, coarsely chopped
5 garlic cloves, chopped
1 tablespoon chopped fresh ginger root
½–1 fresh hot green chili pepper, chopped
1 oz. (30 g). butter
1 teaspoon curry powder
½ teaspoon cumin
seeds of 6 cardamom pods
7 oz. (225 g) cooked or drained tinned chickpeas (garbanzos)
2 teaspoons chickpea (besan) flour (optional)
¾ cup (6 fl. oz., 185 ml) vegetable broth (see p. 15)
1¼ lbs. (625 g) broccoli, cut into bite-sized florets, stems peeled and sliced
¾–1 cup (6–8 fl. oz., 185–250 ml) yogurt
salt and cayenne pepper, to taste
12 oz. (375 g) spaghetti
juice of ½ lemon
2 tablespoons chopped fresh coriander leaves, to serve

Lightly sauté the onion, garlic, ginger root, and chili pepper in the butter until they have softened, then sprinkle in the spices and cook for a moment or two.

Add the chickpeas and chickpea flour (if using), and cook for 2–3 minutes, then stir in the broth and bring to the boil. Add the broccoli and cook until crisp-tender.

Remove the broccoli from the sauce with a slotted spoon, then increase the heat and reduce the sauce until it is very thick. Remove from the heat, stir in the yogurt, and return the broccoli to the pan. Add the salt and cayenne pepper, then cover and keep warm.

Cook the spaghetti in boiling, salted water until *al dente*, then drain.

Toss the pasta with the broccoli sauce; sprinkle with the lemon juice and fresh coriander leaves and serve.

S E R V E S   4

LEFT ♦ *Couscous Pilaf with Shiitake*

Pasta alla Giardino [Pasta from the Garden]

1 onion, chopped
2 garlic cloves, chopped
1 scallion (spring onion), including the green part,
    finely sliced
1 tablespoon chopped fresh parsley
1 oz. (30 g) butter
1–2 zucchini (courgettes), diced
4 fresh artichoke hearts (prepare as on p. 18), cut
    into eighths (or use frozen or tinned)
8 oz. (250 g) fresh or frozen peas
8–10 ripe fresh or tinned tomatoes, diced
1–2 tablespoons tomato paste (purée)
salt and freshly ground black pepper, to taste
pinch of sugar (optional)
1 lb. (500 g) spaghetti
freshly grated Parmesan, pecorino or similar
    cheese, to serve
fresh herbs such as marjoram, basil or oregano,
    to serve

Gently sauté the onion, garlic, scallion, and parsley in half the butter, until they have softened. Add the zucchini and artichoke hearts and cook gently for about 5 minutes.

Add the peas, tomatoes, and tomato paste, plus ¼–⅓ cup (2–3 fl. oz., 60–90 ml) of water and cook over medium to high heat for another few minutes, until the mixture has the consistency of a sauce.

Season with salt and pepper, and sugar (if using).

Cook the spaghetti until *al dente*, then drain. Toss the pasta with the remaining butter, then with the sauce.

Serve immediately, sprinkled with finely grated cheese and a handful of chopped fresh herbs.

SERVES 4–6

Linguine with Roasted Tomatoes, Basil, Garlic, and Pine Nuts

3 tablespoons pine nuts
4 garlic cloves, coarsely chopped
4 tablespoons extra virgin olive oil
large handful of fresh basil leaves, coarsely torn
    or cut up
about 15 small to medium tomatoes, roasted,
    peeled, and diced (see p. 18)
4 tablespoons dry white wine
4 tablespoons vegetable broth (see p. 15)
pinch of sugar, optional
salt and freshly ground black pepper and
    cayenne pepper, to taste
1 lb. (500 g) linguine
freshly grated Parmesan cheese, to serve

Toast the pine nuts in an ungreased heavy skillet (frying pan) over medium heat, tossing and stirring occasionally, until they are golden brown in spots. Do not let them get too brown — they can burn very suddenly. Remove from the heat.

Sauté the garlic in the olive oil until fragrant and golden, then add the basil and the roasted tomatoes and cook over medium to high heat for a minute or so. Add the wine and broth and cook over a high heat until the liquid is reduced in volume by about half. Season with the sugar (if using), salt, pepper, and cayenne pepper.

Meanwhile, cook the pasta until *al dente*, then drain.

Toss the pasta with the sauce and pine nuts, then serve immediately, sprinkled with the Parmesan cheese.

SERVES 4–6

RIGHT ♦ *Pasta alla Giardino (Pasta from the Garden)*

Linguine alla Pizzaiola
[With Tomatoes, Mozzarella, and Basil]

Classic flavors of the Italian summertime.

3 garlic cloves, coarsely chopped

2 tablespoons extra virgin olive oil

8 ripe sweet tomatoes, peeled, seeded, and diced
   (tinned diced tomatoes are acceptable), drained
   of excess juice (reserve the juice)

2 tablespoons tomato paste (purée)

salt and freshly ground black pepper, to taste

12–16 oz. (375–500 g) linguine

6–8 oz. (185–250 g) fresh milky mozzarella cheese,
   cut into large dice

several large handfuls of fresh basil leaves, coarsely
   torn or left whole

Warm the garlic in the olive oil just long enough to bring
out its fragrance. Add the diced tomatoes and tomato
paste and cook for a minute or two, adding some of the
tomato juice if needed. Season with salt and pepper, then
set aside and keep warm.

Cook the linguine in boiling, salted water until
al dente, then drain.

Toss the pasta with the hot sauce and the mozzarella
cheese. Scatter basil over the top and serve immediately.

VARIATION

Breadcrumbs, either toasted or fresh, are very good with
tomato- and basil-dressed pasta. You can omit the
mozzarella if you prefer.

SERVES 4–6

Pasta with Cabbage, Leeks, and
Tomatoes Topped with Cheese

Consummately comforting.

½ head green or white cabbage, thinly sliced

1 leek, coarsely chopped

3–4 garlic cloves, coarsely chopped

1 oz. (30 g) butter, plus extra for tossing with
   the pasta

2 tablespoons flour

1 cup (8 fl. oz., 250 ml) hot (not boiling) milk

1 lb. (500 g) ripe tomatoes, diced, or 1½ tins
   (14 oz., 435 g tins) chopped tomatoes

dried mixed herbs such as herbes de Provence
   or Italian herbs, to taste

salt and freshly ground black pepper, to taste

1 lb. (500 g) spaghetti or other pasta of choice

10 oz. (310 g) mature Cheddar cheese,
   coarsely grated

Sauté the cabbage, leek, and garlic in the butter until the
vegetables have softened. Sprinkle with the flour and
cook for a few minutes, then stir in the milk and cook
over a medium heat until the sauce thickens and the
vegetables are tender. Add the tomatoes and continue
cooking until the mixture becomes a thick, chunky,
vegetable sauce. Season with dried mixed herbs and salt
and black pepper.

Meanwhile, cook the pasta until *al dente,* then drain.
Toss the pasta in a little butter, and then with the sauce.
Top each portion with a generous sprinkling of the
grated cheese, and serve immediately.

SERVES 4–6

Curly Pasta with Curried Soya Mince, Browned Garlic Oil, and Minted Yogurt

This unlikely and absolutely delicious dish is vaguely Middle Eastern in origin. The contrast of flavors and textures is marvellous. Though the recipe looks time-consuming, it is very easy to prepare.

10 garlic cloves, sliced or coarsely chopped
3 fl. oz. (90 ml) extra virgin olive oil
1 cup (8 fl. oz., 250 ml) yogurt
1 teaspoon dried mint, crumbled, or to taste
12–16 oz. (375–500 g) thick twisting pasta such
    as fusilli lunghi, or thick straight pasta such as
    bucatini, broken into shorter lengths

Curried Soya Mince
1 onion, chopped
2 garlic cloves, chopped
1 hot chili pepper, chopped
½ in. (25 mm) piece fresh ginger root, chopped
1 carrot, diced
½ red sweet pepper (capsicum), coarsely chopped
2 tablespoons vegetable or extra virgin olive oil
enough soya mince (textured soy protein) to
    make 1 lb. (500 g) when rehydrated
3–4 chard (silver beet) or outer cabbage leaves,
    blanched and thinly sliced
½ teaspoon curry powder
¼ teaspoon turmeric
¼ teaspoon cumin
pinch of lavender (optional)
1 bouillon (stock) cube
1 oz. (30 g). fresh coriander, coarsely chopped
dash of lemon juice
salt and freshly ground black pepper, to taste

Heat the garlic in the oil in a heavy skillet or frying pan over a medium heat until it is golden. Remove from the heat and set aside.

Mix together the yogurt and mint, and chill.

To make the curried soya mince, sauté the onion, garlic, chili pepper, ginger root, carrot, and sweet pepper in the oil until they have softened, then add the soya mince and cook over a medium heat for a few more minutes, until lightly browned.

Add the chard (or cabbage), curry powder, turmeric,

cumin, lavender (if using), bouillon cube, and enough water to rehydrate the soya mince (follow the instructions on the packet). Cook for 15–20 minutes, until the mince is rehydrated and the mixture has the consistency of a sauce.

Add the coriander leaves, lemon juice, and salt and pepper.

Cook the pasta until *al dente*, then drain.

Serve the pasta tossed with the browned garlic oil, and topped with the curried soya mince and a dollop of minted yogurt.

SERVES 4–6

Spaghetti with Browned Onions, Spinach, and Blue Cheese

A delightfully different pasta dish with the sweet–savory flavor of browned onions, the freshness of lightly cooked spinach, and the salty tang of blue cheese.

6–8 onions, cut into ⅛–¼ in. (3–6 mm) slices
2–3 fl. oz. (60–90 ml) extra virgin olive oil,
    or as needed
12 oz. (375 g) spaghetti
1 bunch spinach leaves, well washed, then torn
    into bite-sized pieces
4–5 oz. (125–155 g) blue cheese, crumbled
freshly ground black pepper, to taste

Brown the onion slices in a heavy skillet (frying pan) with as little of the olive oil as possible, cooking them quickly until they have slightly softened and are brown in spots; they should not be limp and dark brown. Set aside.

Cook the spaghetti until half-cooked, then add the spinach and continue cooking until the pasta is *al dente* and the spinach is tender and bright green. Drain, then toss the pasta and spinach in the remaining olive oil.

Top the pasta and spinach with the onions, then crumble the blue cheese over. Season with pepper and serve immediately.

SERVES 4

Pasta and Green Beans (or Asparagus) with Mascarpone and Breadcrumb Sauce

I often make a few changes to this traditional Italian Alpine dish: asparagus is the vegetable most often used, but I often substitute green beans. As for cheeses, fontina or Gruyère are the usual choice, but I often opt for Parmesan instead.

4 oz. (125 g) stale country-style bread
1 tablespoon oil or ½ oz. (15 g) butter
1 lb. (500 g) pasta of choice
8 oz. (250 g) green or string beans, cut into bite-sized lengths, or asparagus, tough stems broken off and the stalks cut into bite-sized lengths
1½ cups (12 fl. oz., 375 ml) vegetable broth (see p. 15)
5–8 oz. (155–250 g) mascarpone cheese, at room temperature
6 oz. (185 g) fontina or Gruyère cheese, grated, or several heaped tablespoons freshly grated Parmesan cheese
salt and freshly ground black pepper, to taste

Grate the bread then toast the breadcrumbs in the oil or butter in a heavy skillet (frying pan) over low to medium heat. When crisp and golden, remove from the heat.

Cook the pasta until half-cooked. Add the green beans or asparagus and continue to cook until both are *al dente*; drain.

Meanwhile, heat the broth until it bubbles around the edges, then add the breadcrumbs and mascarpone cheese. Stir until the cheese melts creamily into the sauce, then toss the sauce with the pasta and vegetables. Add the second cheese, season with salt and pepper, and serve immediately.

VARIATION

Cauliflower and Farfalle Gratin: Instead of green beans or asparagus, use 1 cauliflower, cut into florets. Blanch the cauliflower, then sauté the florets, after sautéing the breadcrumbs. Use farfalle or another short, chubby-shaped pasta.

Add the cooked cauliflower to the pasta and creamy breadcrumb sauce. Top with additional grated cheese and grill or bake in a hot oven until the cheese has melted.

SERVES 6

Rigatoni and Green Beans with Chorreadas Sauce

Chorreadas is a spicy Bolivian tomato and cheese sauce, seasoned with ginger and turmeric. It is especially good served with thick, robust pasta such as rigatoni and tossed with crisp green beans.

4 onions, diced
2 tablespoons extra virgin olive oil
8 oz. (250 g) ripe tomatoes, diced
12 oz. (375 g) rigatoni
8 oz. (250 g) fresh or frozen green or string beans, cut into bite-sized pieces
½–1 fresh chili pepper, chopped
½–¾ teaspoon turmeric
¼ teaspoon cumin
pinch of sugar (optional)
½ cup (4 fl. oz., 125 ml) Greek-style yogurt, or sour cream
12–14 oz. (375–435 g) white cheese such as Cheddar, fontina, Jarlsberg, etc., cubed
salt and freshly ground black pepper or cayenne pepper, to taste
½–1 oz. (15–30 g) butter, at room temperature
pinch of dried ginger
1 garlic clove, chopped
1 tablespoon chopped fresh coriander leaves

Sweat the onions in the olive oil until they have softened. Add the tomatoes then sauté together for about 3 minutes. Do not stir the mixture into a sauce — let it remain at an almost relish-like consistency.

Meanwhile, cook the rigatoni until half-cooked. Add the green beans and continue cooking until both pasta and beans are *al dente*, then drain.

Add the chili, turmeric, cumin, sugar (if using), yogurt, and cheese to the onion and tomato mixture. Cook over a medium heat, stirring all the time, until the cheese melts. Season with salt and pepper or cayenne pepper.

Toss the pasta and green beans with the sauce, then toss in the butter, ginger, and garlic. Serve immediately, garnished with the chopped coriander leaves.

SERVES 4–6

RIGHT ♦ *Pasta with Green Beans (or Asparagus) with Mascarpone and Breadcrumb Sauce*

Farfalle or Penne with Sun-dried Tomato and Goat Cheese Purée

Since this sauce needs no cooking it is almost like a pesto in simplicity of preparation and freshness of flavor. Try it on pasta stuffed with mushrooms, spinach, or other vegetables strong enough to stand up to the sun-dried tomatoes and goat cheese.

3 garlic cloves, chopped
15 oil-marinated sun-dried tomatoes, coarsely chopped
5 oz. (155 g) goat cheese, crumbled
large pinch of fresh or dried thyme
2 tablespoons extra virgin olive oil
12 oz. (375 g) farfalle or penne
15 fresh whole basil leaves

In a blender (liquidizer) or food processor, combine the garlic, sun-dried tomatoes, goat cheese, thyme, and olive oil. Process to a creamy pinkish paste, then set aside.

Cook the pasta until *al dente*, then drain.

Toss the pasta with the purée, sprinkle with the basil, then serve immediately.

SERVES 4

Lumache or Penne with Ricotta Cheese and Black Olives

1 onion, chopped
4 garlic cloves, chopped
1–2 fl. oz. (30–60 ml) extra virgin olive oil
1 tablespoon chopped fresh rosemary
freshly ground black pepper, to taste
12–14 oz. (375–435 g) ricotta cheese
about 25–35 black olives (Greek, kalamata, Niçoise, or oil-cured), pitted and diced
1 lb. (500 g) lumache, penne, or other chubby-shaped pasta
freshly grated Parmesan cheese, to serve

Lightly sauté the onion and garlic in the olive oil until they have just softened.

Remove from the heat and add the rosemary, black pepper, ricotta, and olives. Set aside.

Cook the pasta until *al dente*, then drain. Toss the pasta with the sauce, then with Parmesan cheese. Serve immediately.

SERVES 4–6

Spaghetti with Toasted Cumin and Simmered Garlic in Tangy Cheese Sauce

Greek-style yogurt adds a tangy quality to this cumin-scented cheese sauce. As untraditional and surprising as the recipe may sound, it makes a delicious bowlful.

10 garlic cloves, peeled but left whole
1 cup (8 fl. oz., 250 ml) vegetable broth (see p. 15)
12 oz. (375 g) spaghetti
½ teaspoon cumin seeds, or to taste
3–4 tablespoons Greek-style yogurt or sour cream
6 oz. (185 g) white cheese such as fontina,
    Cheddar, Jarlsberg, etc., diced or grated
freshly ground black pepper, to taste

Simmer the garlic cloves in the stock for 15–20 minutes, until they are tender. Set aside.

Cook the pasta until *al dente*, then drain.

Meanwhile, prepare the sauce: lightly toast the cumin seeds in an ungreased heavy skillet (frying pan) over a medium heat for a minute or two, until they are fragrant. Do not let them burn.

Add the garlic cloves and half of the vegetable broth, heat through, then add the yogurt or sour cream and cheese. (Do not worry about the lumpy appearance of the sauce: it is the soft garlic cloves, and they make a nice surprise when bitten into.) Thin with remaining broth if needed, or reserve this for another purpose.

Toss the pasta with the sauce and serve immediately, seasoned with black pepper.

SERVES 4

Pasta with Sautéed Onions and Vignottes Cheese

Sautéed onions combine with pungent Vignottes cheese for pasta with a French accent. Vignottes has a delicate heart, with a rind that gets rather stinky as it grows older.

4 oz. (125 g) stale, crusty country-style bread,
    coarsely grated into crumbs
1½ oz. (45 g) butter
3 onions, chopped
2 garlic cloves, chopped
½ cup (4 fl. oz., 125 ml) light (single) cream
    (optional)
11 oz. (340 g) Vignottes cheese
1 lb. (500 g) spaghetti or fettuccine
salt and freshly ground black pepper, to taste

Toast the breadcrumbs in about half the butter until they are golden and crisp. Remove from the pan and set aside.

In the remaining butter, lightly sauté the onions and garlic until they have softened and are lightly browned, then add the cream (if using). Cook for a minute or two, until the sauce has thickened.

Cut the cheese into small pieces. If the rind is very pungent, remove some or all of it. Toss the cheese into the hot pan, swirl it through, then remove from the heat.

Meanwhile, cook the pasta until *al dente,* then drain. Toss the pasta with the onion and cheese mixture, and season with salt and pepper. Sprinkle with the toasted breadcrumbs, and serve immediately.

SERVES 4–6

LEFT ♦ *Farfalle or Penne with Sun-dried Tomato and Goat Cheese Purée*

Pasta with Chickpeas and Garlic–Rosemary–Lemon Sauce

Browning garlic then simmering it with rosemary, broth, and lemon juice makes a tangy sauce for macaroni and nutty chickpeas (garbanzos). Season with hot chili pepper for a spicy accent.

8 garlic cloves, coarsely chopped
2 tablespoons extra virgin olive oil
½ oz. (15 g) butter
2 tablespoons coarsely chopped fresh rosemary
½ cup (4 fl. oz., 125 ml) vegetable broth (see p. 15)
several leaves chopped fresh spinach, or
    1 tablespoon cooked spinach, chopped (optional)
2 tablespoons lemon juice
14 oz. (435 g) cooked or drained tinned chickpeas
    (garbanzos)
12 oz. (375 g) short pasta
cayenne pepper or hot chili pepper flakes, to taste
salt and freshly ground black pepper, to taste

Cook the garlic in the olive oil and butter over a medium heat until the garlic is golden. Add the rosemary, stir through, then add the broth and cook until the liquid is reduced by about half.

Add the spinach (if using) and the lemon juice, and cook over a medium heat until the sauce is strongly flavored and almost syrupy. Add the chickpeas and set aside.

Meanwhile, cook the pasta until *al dente*, then drain.

Toss the pasta with the sauce. Season with cayenne pepper or hot chili pepper flakes, and salt and pepper, then serve immediately, adding a squeeze of lemon juice at the last minute if needed.

SERVES 4–6

Pappardelle with Broccoli and Red Beans

Wide strips of noodles tossed with a brash and satisfying mixture of broccoli, tomatoes, and red beans is a typical dish from the Mezzogiorno (the south) of Italy. Any fairly large pasta shape is good with this hearty bean and broccoli mixture: the hollow tubes called bucatini, rotelle or penne.

3–4 garlic cloves, finely chopped
3 tablespoons extra virgin olive oil
1¼ lbs. (625 g) broccoli, cut into bite-sized florets,
    the stems peeled and sliced
5 fresh or tinned tomatoes, chopped
1½ cups (12 fl. oz., 375 ml) tomato purée (passata)
pinch of sugar (optional)
14 oz. (435 g) cooked or drained tinned white
    kidney beans, or cannellini beans
1 lb. (500 g) pappardelle, or other pasta shape
    of choice
freshly grated Parmesan cheese, to serve

Lightly sauté the garlic in the olive oil until the garlic is fragrant and barely colored, then add the broccoli. Cook over a medium heat for a minute or two, then add the tomatoes and tomato purée and continue cooking for a few minutes, until the mixture has the consistency of a sauce. Increase the heat if it is too liquid. Add the sugar if the sauce is too acidic.

Add the beans and simmer. Meanwhile, cook the pasta until *al dente*. Drain the pasta and serve it with the sauce (and Parmesan cheese as desired).

SERVES 6

RIGHT ♦ *Pasta with Chickpeas and Garlic–Rosemary–Lemon Sauce*

Far Eastern Pasta

*While the old belief that pasta
was brought to Italy from China by Marco Polo has been pretty much debunked,
there is no doubt that noodles have been eaten in the Far East for a very long time. Traditional Chinese,
Japanese, Burmese, Vietnamese, Thai, and other Southeast Asian pasta dishes abound, and well they should
— their bland quality pairs so well with strong and pungent Far Eastern flavors:
soy, sesame, chili pepper, lime, and so on.*

◆ ◆ ◆

*Far Eastern pasta is not always made
from wheat; rice, buckwheat, mung beans, and potato flour are among the various ingredients used
to make Asian noodles. They have slightly different qualities from Italian and other Western pasta, and use
different seasoning ingredients: sharp and savory, pungent sauces and soups, rather than the more
Mediterranean-flavored or creamy sauces of the West. I have grouped these Asian or Far Eastern dishes
together in this chapter, although there are a number scattered throughout other chapters.*

◆ ◆ ◆

Southeast Asian Rice Noodle Broth with Lime, Chili Peppers, Salad, and Peanuts

This outstanding soup performs a balancing act of aromas, flavors, and textures; its chili pepper heat and lightness make it particularly good summer fare, and it has the bonus of being quick and easy to prepare.

12 oz. (375 g) dried, wide rice noodles, preferably Vietnamese

4 cups (1¾ imp. pints, 1 litre) vegetable broth (see p. 15)

2 garlic cloves, coarsely chopped

3–4 scallions (spring onions), thinly sliced

1 cucumber, roughly chopped

2 tablespoons chopped fresh coriander leaves

2 tablespoons chopped fresh mint leaves

3–4 tablespoons coarsely chopped dry-roasted peanuts

2 fresh green medium–hot chili peppers, thinly sliced

1 lime, cut into wedges

Soak the noodles in cold water for 10 minutes. Drain, then plunge into boiling water for 3–5 minutes; drain.

Heat the broth with the garlic, then add the drained noodles and cook until heated through.

Serve immediately, garnished with the remaining ingredients.

SERVES 4

South Pacific–East Asian Coconut Soup with Chinese Egg Noodles, Green Beans, and Water Chestnuts

This broth is very rich yet clean-tasting, with a complexity that belies its simplicity. I like to sip the mild creamy soup first, then when I reach the noodles, add a squeeze of lemon or lime juice and a shake of hot pepper or Tabasco sauce.

12 oz. (375 g) Chinese egg noodles, either fresh or dried
soy sauce and/or sesame oil to season the noodles
3 scallions (spring onions), thinly sliced
10–15 water chestnuts, diced
2 heaped tablespoons coarsely chopped fresh coriander leaves
1 egg, lightly beaten
2 cups (16 fl. oz., 500 ml) vegetable broth (see p. 15)
2 oz. (60 g) creamed coconut in block form (or reduce the broth 1 cup (8 fl. oz., 250 ml) and use 1 cup (8 fl. oz., 250 ml) unsweetened coconut milk or cream)
handful of green beans, cut into bite-sized lengths
cayenne pepper to taste
1 lime or lemon, cut into wedges

Cook the noodles until *al dente*; drain and rinse with cold water. Season with a few splashes of soy sauce and/or sesame oil, then mix with the scallions, water chestnuts, coriander leaves, and egg; set aside. (This may be done up to a day in advance and kept covered in the refrigerator.)

Combine the vegetable broth, coconut milk or cream (if using a block, let it melt in as the broth heats) and green beans. Bring to the boil. Beans should be bright green and the broth should be creamy.

Add the noodle mixture to the soup and stir to combine, heating for a minute or two to cook the egg.

Serve immediately, each portion sprinkled with cayenne pepper and accompanied by a wedge of lime or lemon to squeeze in.

SERVES 4–6

East-West Pasta Primavera

Any vegetables in season would be delicious in this East–West potful: try carrots sliced on the diagonal, Napa cabbage (Chinese leaves) cut into strips, blanched sliced spring greens, sliced zucchini (courgettes), and so on.

12 oz. (375 g) lasagne, or 1 packet fresh wonton noodles
1 tablespoon sesame oil, plus extra for seasoning
2–3 scallions (spring onions), thinly sliced
3–4 garlic cloves, chopped
½-in. (1.25-cm) piece fresh ginger root, chopped
2 tablespoons vegetable oil
10–12 oz. (310–375 g) broccoli, cut into bite-sized pieces
4 oz. (125 g) asparagus, cut into bite-sized lengths
1 red sweet pepper (capsicum), cut into strips
½ cup (4 fl. oz., 125 ml) vegetable broth (see p. 15)
1 tablespoon cornstarch (cornflour), mixed into a paste with a little water
soy sauce to taste
2 tablespoons chopped fresh coriander leaves

Cook the lasagne or noodles until just tender. Drain, rinse in cold water, toss in the sesame oil and set aside.

In a large skillet (frying pan) or wok, stir-fry half the scallions, garlic, and ginger root in 1 tablespoon of the oil; add the broccoli and cook until crisp-tender. Remove and set aside.

In the remaining oil stir-fry the remaining scallions, garlic, and ginger root. Add the asparagus and red sweet pepper and cook until just tender. Remove and set aside.

Mix the broth and cornstarch until smooth, then pour into the hot pan or wok and stir together until it thickens. Add the lasagne or wonton noodles and the vegetables, then toss to heat through. Remove from the heat, season with soy sauce and sesame oil, then serve immediately, sprinkled with the coriander leaves.

SERVES 4–6

PREVIOUS PAGE ♦ *South Pacific–East Asian Coconut Soup with Chinese Egg Noodles, Green Beans, and Water Chestnuts (left), East–West Pasta Primavera (top), and Mee Goreng (right)*
LEFT ♦ *Southeast Asian Rice Noodle Broth with Lime, Chili Peppers, Salad, and Peanuts*

Mee Goreng

Mee Goreng is a spicy noodle dish from the street stalls and coffee shops of Singapore. These are run by Indians, and although Mee Goreng has none of the curry spices one usually associates with foods from the Indian subcontinent and is completely unknown in any part of India, in Singapore and Malaysia it is known as Indian-style noodles.

6–8 oz. (185–250 g) Chinese-style dried noodles
2 teaspoons soy sauce
5–6 garlic cloves, chopped
3 tablespoons vinegar
1 teaspoon Tabasco sauce or other hot pepper sauce
1 tablespoon sugar
3 tablespoons tomato ketchup
2 tablespoons vegetable oil, more if needed
¼ green or white cabbage, cut into small dice
6 scallions (spring onions), thinly sliced
1 tomato, diced
several 1-in. (2.5-cm) squares deep-fried tofu, cut into ¼-in. (6-mm) slices (optional)
10–15 tinned, or fresh and blanched, water chestnuts, diced
2 eggs, lightly beaten
4 oz. (125 g) bean sprouts
3–4 tablespoons crunchy roasted peanuts or about 2 tablespoons crisp-fried shallot flakes
1 fresh green chili pepper, cut into thin strips
2 tablespoons fresh coriander leaves
¼ cucumber, halved lengthwise then thinly sliced
lemon or lime wedges

Cook the noodles in rapidly boiling salted water with half the soy sauce. Drain and rinse with cold water then set aside.

Make a sauce by combining the remaining soy sauce with 1 clove of the chopped garlic, the vinegar, Tabasco or other hot sauce, sugar, and tomato ketchup. Set aside.

Heat about three-quarters of the oil in a wok or heavy skillet (frying pan), add the remaining garlic and sauté quickly until golden. Over high heat, add the cabbage, half the scallions, the tomato, tofu (if using), and the water chestnuts. Stir-fry for about 30 to 60 seconds or until crisp-tender.

Add the noodles and the sauce, toss over the heat and, if using a large wok, push the mixture to one side; if there is not enough room, transfer the mixture to a platter or casserole dish and keep warm.

Add the remaining oil to the pan and pour in the eggs, stirring them until scrambled, then add the bean sprouts and toss until wilted.

Combine the noodle mixture with the eggs and bean sprouts and serve immediately, topped with the peanuts or crisp shallot flakes, the chili pepper strips, coriander leaves, cucumber, and remaining scallions. Serve accompanied by lemon or lime wedges.

SERVES 3–4

Pasta with East–West Pesto

Fresh coriander and chili peppers are pounded with peanuts into a pesto-like seasoning paste and tossed with rice noodles.

3 garlic cloves, chopped
2–3 fresh green chili peppers, chopped
3 tablespoons peanut butter or coarsely chopped roasted peanuts
1 oz. (30 g) fresh coriander leaves, chopped
1 oz. (30 g) fresh mint leaves, chopped, or additional coriander leaves
pinch of sugar
salt to taste
juice of ½ lemon or lime
soy sauce, to taste
12 oz. (375 g) rice noodles (also called rice sticks or rice vermicelli)
sesame oil, to taste

In a liquidizer (blender) or food processor, process the garlic, chili peppers, peanut butter or chopped peanuts, coriander, mint (if using), sugar, salt, and lemon or lime juice. Add a little soy sauce if needed to get the right consistency.

Soak and cook the noodles according to directions on the packet, then drain and toss with soy sauce and sesame oil to taste. Serve each portion topped with a few spoonfuls of the thick green paste, and toss together.

SERVES 4–6

RIGHT ♦ *Cold Buckwheat Soba with Snow Peas and Water Chestnuts*

Cold Buckwheat Soba with Snow Peas and Water Chestnuts

375 g (12 oz.) buckwheat soba, about the same width as fettuccine

4 oz. (125 g) snow peas (mangetout)

2 tablespoons sesame oil

1 tablespoon vegetable oil

3 scallions (spring onions), thinly sliced

2–3 tablespoons soy sauce, preferably dark

dash of hot sauce, such as Tabasco or hot chili pepper oil

1 tablespoon lemon juice, balsamic vinegar, or Chinese black vinegar

2 teaspoons sugar, or to taste

salt to taste

10 water chestnuts, tinned, or fresh and blanched, sliced

2 tablespoons toasted sesame seeds or slivered almonds (optional)

Cook the buckwheat soba until almost tender then add the snow peas and cook for a minute or two longer until the noodles are *al dente* and the vegetables are bright green and crisp-tender. Drain and rinse with cold water.

Mix with the sesame oil, vegetable oil, scallions, soy sauce, hot sauce, lemon juice (or vinegar), sugar, and salt to taste. Add the water chestnuts and chill for at least an hour. Taste for seasoning. Garnish with the sesame seeds or almonds (if using).

SERVES 4

Crisp-fried Rice Noodle Cloud Over Spicy–Sweet Mixed Vegetable Stir-fry

Thin rice noodles fry up into a crispy, light, cloud-like mass, making a delightful counterpoint to savory stir-fries or tangy fresh vegetable salads.

4 oz. (125 g) thin rice noodles (also called rice sticks or rice vermicelli)
vegetable oil for deep-frying, plus a very small amount for stir-frying
1–2 onions, thinly sliced
3 garlic cloves, chopped
1 tablespoon chopped fresh ginger root
1 green sweet pepper (capsicum), diced
1 red sweet pepper (capsicum), diced
handful of green beans, snow peas (mangetout), or asparagus, cut into 2-in. (5-cm) lengths
10–15 mushrooms, quartered
1 zucchini (courgette), sliced on the diagonal
4 oz. (125 g) water chestnuts, quartered or sliced
handful of bean sprouts
½ cup (4 fl. oz., 125 ml) hoisin sauce
½ cup (4 fl. oz., 125 ml) vegetable broth (see p. 15)
1 tablespoon cornstarch (cornflour)
1 tablespoon soy sauce, or to taste
1 tablespoon sugar
hot chili pepper seasoning, to taste
1–2 tablespoons fresh coriander leaves

Deep-fry the dry rice noodles in very small batches in medium hot oil. It will take only a few minutes for them to sizzle and expand dramatically, becoming light and crisp. Do not let the noodles become golden; when they are crispy light and still white, but no longer tough or crunchy, remove with a slotted spoon and drain on absorbent paper, then set aside.

In a wok or heavy skillet (frying pan), stir-fry the onions, garlic, ginger root, and green and red sweet peppers in very little oil. When tender-crunchy remove from the pan and set aside, then stir-fry in separate batches the green beans or snow peas or asparagus with the mushrooms, and the zucchini and the water chestnuts with the bean sprouts. Set all the vegetables aside.

Mix the hoisin sauce with the broth, cornstarch, soy sauce, sugar, and hot chili pepper seasoning. Pour into the hot wok and stir until thickened; return the vegetables to the pan and toss with the sauce.

Serve immediately, arranging the vegetables on a platter, topping them with a halo of crisp rice noodles and finished with a sprinkling of coriander leaves.

SERVES 4

Japanese-style Noodles in Broth Topped with Savory Custard

The fat, thick noodles — called udon — are delicious in this Japanese noodle snack, but as they are usually available only in Japanese, Chinese, or other Far Eastern grocery stores, I often substitute dried Chinese-style egg noodles, which are readily available.

3–4 oz. (90–125 g) dried egg noodles, or fresh udon
1–1¼ cups (8–10 fl oz., 250–310 ml) vegetable broth (see p. 15)
1 egg, lightly beaten
½ teaspoon soy sauce
1 scallion (spring onion), thinly sliced

Cook the noodles until just tender; drain.

Heat the broth to boiling; remove from the heat and keep hot. Combine the egg with the soy sauce and scallion.

Add the noodles to the hot broth, then pour the egg mixture over the top. Do not stir together, but let it more or less float on top of the soup. Cover and cook over low to medium heat until the egg mixture is steamed to firmness.

Serve immediately, with extra soy sauce to taste.

SERVES 1–2

RIGHT ♦ *Crisp-fried Rice Noodle Cloud Over Spicy–Sweet Mixed Vegetable Stir-fry*

Spicy Black Bean Chow Mein with Stir-fried Cabbage and Shiitake

Chow mein is quite familiar to anyone with a penchant for Chinese food, but this Cantonese speciality is only one of a wide variety of Chinese noodle dishes. A chewy-crisp pillow of noodles combined with stir-fried vegetables and aromatics, chow mein can be made with anything from your garden, and seasoned with a vast array of flavors. Here the vegetables are a combination of the humble and the exotic: cabbage, carrots, and bean sprouts, with a scattering of dried shiitake and tree cloud fungus. It is spiced with fermented black beans, fresh chili pepper, and coriander.

12 oz. (375 g) dried or fresh Chinese egg noodles
3 tablespoons vegetable oil
10 dried shiitake (Chinese black mushrooms)
2–3 large tree cloud fungus
3 garlic cloves, chopped
¼-in. (6-mm) piece fresh ginger root, chopped
1 carrot, diced
½ green or white cabbage, diced
pinch of sugar
4 oz. (125 g) bean sprouts
2 tablespoons fermented black beans
1 tablespoon cornstarch (cornflour)
¾ cup (6 fl. oz., 185 ml) vegetable broth
   (see p. 15)
½–1 fresh chili pepper, thinly sliced, or cayenne
   pepper or other hot seasoning, to taste
soy sauce, to taste
2 teaspoons sesame oil, or to taste
3 scallions (spring onions), thinly sliced
2–3 tablespoons whole fresh coriander leaves

Boil the noodles until just tender; drain and rinse with cold water then drain well again.

Rub a baking sheet (tray) with 1 tablespoon of the oil and spread the cooked noodles evenly over it. Bake in the oven at 400°F (200°C) for 20 minutes, then turn over and brown for another 10 minutes. The noodles will stick together in a crispy, golden, sheet-like pancake. (They may be prepared up to two days in advance, and kept at room temperature, away from moisture. To reheat and recrisp, place in the oven at 250°F (120°C) for about 20 minutes.)

Rehydrate the shiitake and tree cloud fungus in hot (not boiling) water to cover, as described on page 17, reserving the soaking liquid for another use (for this recipe, you may soak them together instead of separately). Cut the stems off the shiitake and discard. Slice the shiitake into halves, or smaller pieces if they are very large, and slice the tree cloud fungus into thin strips. Set aside.

In a wok or skillet (frying pan) stir-fry the garlic, ginger root, carrot, and soaked shiitake in 1 tablespoon of the oil, then add the cabbage and sugar and stir-fry for about 30 seconds, or until the cabbage wilts slightly. Remove from the pan.

Add the remaining oil to the pan, if needed, and quickly stir-fry the bean sprouts until just wilted. Remove from the pan and add to the cabbage mixture.

Lightly crush the fermented black beans with the back of a spoon on the handle of a Chinese cleaver. Mix with the cornstarch, broth, and chili pepper or other hot seasoning, and add to the pan. Cook until thickened, then return the vegetables to the sauce and toss through. Add the noodles, broken up into several pieces, and heat through for a few seconds.

Serve on a platter, sprinkled with the soy sauce, sesame oil, scallions, and fresh coriander leaves.

VARIATION
Black Bean Chow Mein with Vegetables and Tofu: Replace the cabbage with green beans, cut into bite-sized lengths, zucchini (courgettes) cut into matchsticks, and diced firm or crisp-fried tofu.

SERVES 4

LEFT ♦ *Spicy Black Bean Chow Mein with Stir-fried Cabbage and Shiitake*

Coconut Curry with Rice Noodles, Shiitake, and Water Chestnuts

This easily prepared, somewhat soupy noodle dish has a whiff of curry and the richness of coconut, paired with the earthy flavor of shiitake (Chinese black mushrooms). You can vary the dish by adding a little broccoli or asparagus.

15 dried shiitake (Chinese black mushrooms)
4 cups (1¾ pints, 1 litre) hot (not boiling) water
13 oz. (405 g) thin rice noodles (also called rice sticks or rice vermicelli)
2 vegetable bouillon (stock) cubes
4 oz. (125 g) coconut cream in block form (or substitute unsweetened coconut milk for half the water)
10–15 fresh blanched, or drained tinned, water chestnuts, diced
½ teaspoon curry powder, or to taste, plus a little extra for garnish

Rehydrate the shiitake in the hot water as described on page 17, reserving the soaking liquid. Remove and discard the stems, then thinly slice the caps and set aside.

Soak the rice noodles in cold water for approximately 15 minutes. Drain then cook in boiling water for a few minutes only, until just tender. Drain and rinse with cold water. Set aside.

Heat the shiitake soaking liquid with the bouillon cubes, coconut cream, water chestnuts, curry powder, and shiitake. Cook for a few minutes, until the liquid thickens slightly. Add the noodles and serve immediately, sprinkled lightly with extra curry powder.

VARIATION
Rice Noodles with Shiitake and Tomatoes: Follow the recipe above, but heat the sauce in a skillet (frying pan) instead of a saucepan. Add 2 diced tomatoes to the sauce and cook over medium heat until the liquid is reduced and very thick. This will be a dryish noodle dish now, not a soup. Add the noodles to the sauce and toss together for a moment on the heat. Serve immediately, each portion sprinkled with a generous amount of thinly sliced scallions (spring onions).

SERVES 4–6

Broccoli Chow Fun

Chow fun are sold in Chinese grocery stores. They are fat, soft, rolled sheets of rice noodles and are utterly delicious, even if served just with a drizzle of sesame oil, soy sauce, and scallions (spring onions). They are also good stir-fried with any number of vegetables and sauces. This is a variation on a dish I used to eat in San Francisco's Chinatown late at night, when the rest of the city was asleep but my favorite Chinese restaurant was wide awake and very busy.

3 tablespoons sesame seeds
1 lb (500 g) chow fun
3 garlic cloves, chopped
1–2 teaspoons chopped fresh ginger root
2–3 tablespoons vegetable oil
1–2 bunches broccoli, cut into bite-sized florets, stems peeled and sliced
4 oz. (125 g) bean sprouts (optional)
2 tablespoons sherry
2 teaspoons cornstarch (cornflour)
2 tablespoons soy sauce, preferably dark
2 tablespoons vegetable broth (see p. 15)
2 tablespoons sesame oil
2 scallions (spring onions), chopped

Toast the sesame seeds in an ungreased heavy skillet (frying pan) over low to medium heat, turning occasionally until fragrant and golden brown; set aside.

Cut the chow fun into noodle shapes. (As it will be shaped like a large, fat, rolled pancake, cut it into strips about 1½ in. (4 cm) wide, then unroll.) Set aside.

Heat the garlic and ginger root in half the oil in a wok or heavy skillet (frying pan), then stir-fry the broccoli until crisp-tender and bright green. Remove from the wok and reserve. If using bean sprouts, stir-fry quickly then remove from the wok and set aside.

Mix together the sherry, cornstarch, soy sauce, and vegetable broth. Set aside. Heat the remaining oil until hot but not smoking. Add the chow fun and stir-fry for 2–3 minutes. Remove from the wok, add the sauce and stir until thickened, then return the chow fun and reserved vegetables to the wok and heat through.

Serve immediately, drizzled with the sesame oil, and sprinkled with the scallions and toasted sesame seeds.

SERVES 4

Southeast Asian Rice Noodles with Ginger-Garlic Green Beans and Peanut Sauce

This was inspired by a dish I enjoyed at the table of London cookery writer and illustrator, Leslie Forbes. She served the noodles as a side dish, but I have served them since as a central dish accompanied by a selection of crunchy salad vegetables, such as diced cucumbers sprinkled with cayenne pepper, diced red sweet peppers, crisp-tender carrot slices in sesame oil and rice vinegar, and, perhaps, coarsely chopped peanuts.

12 oz. (375 g) dried rice noodles, about ¼-in. (6-mm) wide (also called rice sticks or rice vermicelli)
8 oz. (250 g) peanut butter (either smooth or crunchy)
½ cup (4 fl. oz., 125 ml) coconut milk or 1–2 oz. (30–60 g) coconut cream dissolved in ½ cup (4 fl. oz., 125 ml) water
cayenne pepper and salt, to taste
1 tablespoon sugar or honey, or to taste
juice of 1 lime, or to taste
5 garlic cloves, coarsely chopped
½-in. (1.25-cm) piece fresh ginger root, chopped
1 tablespoon vegetable oil
8 oz. (250 g) green beans, cut into 2-in. (5-cm) lengths (if not young and tender, blanch first)
2 tablespoons coarsely chopped fresh coriander leaves

Soak the rice noodles in cold water and cook according to the instructions on the packet; drain and set aside.

Combine the peanut butter and coconut milk in a pan and heat gently until melted; stir to mix well then remove from the heat. Season with cayenne pepper, salt, sugar or honey, and lime juice. Set aside.

Stir-fry the garlic and ginger root in the vegetable oil until softened and fragrant; add the green beans and stir-fry together for a minute or two until crisp-tender. Season with salt.

Add the noodles to the green beans, toss through once or twice, then serve on a platter, topped with the peanut sauce and sprinkled with fresh coriander leaves.

SERVES 4–6

Chinese Noodles with Spicy Peanut Butter Sauce and Salad

This makes a lovely summer meal, a first course, or even picnic fare.

1 teaspoon Szechuan (Sichuan) peppercorns
6 garlic cloves, chopped
2 teaspoons chopped fresh ginger root
4 tablespoons peanut butter
2 tablespoons tahini
⅓ cup (3 fl. oz., 90 ml) strong brewed tea
¼ cup (2 fl. oz., 60 ml) soy sauce or to taste
2 tablespoons tomato ketchup
2 tablespoons dry sherry
4 tablespoons sesame oil
1½ tablespoons wine vinegar
2 oz. (60 g) sugar or to taste
1 teaspoon chili pepper oil or about ½ teaspoon cayenne pepper
1 lb (500 g) thin Chinese egg noodles
½ cucumber, diced
1 carrot, grated
4 scallions (spring onions), thinly sliced
handful of bean sprouts, blanched (optional)
3 tablespoons chopped fresh coriander leaves

Lightly toast the Szechuan peppercorns in an ungreased heavy skillet (frying pan), then crush coarsely either in a mortar and pestle or with a rolling pin.

In a food processor or liquidizer (blender) combine the peppercorns with the garlic, ginger root, peanut butter, tahini, tea, soy sauce (reserving a little to toss with the noodles), tomato ketchup, sherry, half the sesame oil, wine vinegar, sugar, and chili pepper oil or cayenne pepper and blend to a smooth sauce.

Cook the noodles then drain and rinse in cold water. Toss with the reserved soy sauce and remaining sesame oil and set aside.

Serve the noodles at room temperature or chilled, with the peanut sauce and cucumber, carrot, scallions, bean sprouts (if using) and fresh coriander leaves.

SERVES 6

Chinese Breakfast Noodles

Tender noodles, freshly cooked and glistening with a splash of soy sauce and sesame oil, are a traditional Chinese breakfast food, dispensed by street stalls. Rice noodles are often used, but fresh wonton noodles or pasta make an excellent substitute. Toppings might include crunchy, toasted sesame seeds or a drizzle of fiery hot chili pepper oil. This recipe gives my favorite combination: sesame oil, soy sauce, and scallions (spring onions), with a sprinkling of crushed peanuts as a last-minute consideration.

12 oz. (375 g) wonton noodles
1–2 tablespoons soy sauce, to taste
2–3 tablespoons sesame oil, to taste
dash of hot sauce, such as Tabasco or chili pepper
   oil (optional)
4–6 scallions (spring onions), thinly sliced
1–2 tablespoons coarsely crushed or chopped
   roasted peanuts (optional)

Cook the wonton noodles in boiling water until just tender (take care when you drop them into the water that they do not stick together in one large chunk); drain.

Season with the soy sauce, sesame oil, and hot chili pepper sauce, if using. Top with the scallions and peanuts, if using, and serve immediately.

SERVES 4

Vietnamese-style Tomato Broth with Cellophane Noodles and Bean Sprouts

Very light yet brightly flavored, this soup makes a refreshing summer supper or winter first course.

2 oz. (60 g) cellophane noodles
5 scallions (spring onions), thinly sliced
1–2 tablespoons vegetable oil
6–8 fresh or tinned tomatoes, chopped
4 cups (1¾ imp. pints, 1 litre) vegetable broth
cayenne pepper to taste
2 handfuls bean sprouts
wedges of lime
3 tablespoons coarsely chopped peanuts

Put the noodles in a bowl and pour over hot, but not boiling, water to cover. Leave for 10 minutes or until softened. Drain and rinse in cold water, then cut into bite-sized strands; set aside.

Lightly sauté the scallions in the oil until softened; add the tomatoes and cook for about 5 minutes. Add the broth, bring to the boil, then add the noodles and simmer for 5–10 minutes or until richly flavored. Season with cayenne pepper. Just before serving, add the bean sprouts and heat through.

Serve each portion sprinkled with the peanuts and accompanied by wedges of lime.

SERVES 4

Spicy Rice Noodle Snack from the Streets of Hong Kong

Just one of the endless noodle dishes ladled up by the street vendors of Hong Kong. They reach into a steamy cauldron, lift out a portion of hot noodles, splash on a little sauce and sprinkle on a garnish and you immediately have a spicy treat.

8 oz. (250 g) dried, flat rice noodles, about ⅛ in.
   (3 mm) wide or 12 oz. (375 g) fresh rice noodles
2 tablespoons hoisin sauce
2 teaspoons chili bean sauce
pinch of sugar, optional
1 tablespoon sesame oil
1–1½ tablespoons soy sauce
1–2 tablespoons fresh coriander leaves (optional)
2 tablespoons toasted sesame seeds (optional)

If using dried rice noodles, soak first for 15 minutes to soften. Cook the soaked or fresh rice noodles until just tender; drain.

Stir together the hoisin sauce, hot bean sauce, sugar (if using), sesame oil, and soy sauce.

Serve the hot noodles topped with the sauce and sprinkled with the fresh coriander leaves and sesame seeds (if using).

SERVES 2–4

LEFT ♦ *Spicy Rice Noodle Snack from the Streets of Hong Kong (top), and Chinese Breakfast Noodles (bottom)*

Panthe Kaukswe (Burmese Noodles with Curry Sauce and Assorted Toppings)

Chickpea flour (besan or gram flour) has a nutty flavor and is almost as high in protein as soy flour. It is used throughout India and parts of the Far East, especially Burma, where it forms the basis for this sauce, Burma's national dish. Panthe Kaukswe can be made with any sort of Far Eastern noodles: cellophane, rice, mung bean threads, or egg noodles. The spicy sauce is splashed on and garnishes are added at the table, so no two bites are ever the same. The sauce is not only easily prepared a day ahead but it tastes best that way too.

4 onions, chopped
6–8 garlic cloves, chopped
1½ tablespoons chopped fresh ginger root
1 teaspoon turmeric
1 teaspoon curry powder
1 stalk lemon grass, peeled, cut into 2-in. (5-cm) lengths, and slightly crushed
generous pinch of cayenne pepper or hot red chili pepper flakes
2 tablespoons vegetable oil
1 tablespoon sesame oil
2 tablespoons chickpea flour (besan)
2 cups (16 fl. oz., 500 ml) coconut milk, or block of coconut cream dissolved in 2 cups (16 fl. oz., 500 ml) hot water
1 cup (8 fl. oz., 250 ml) vegetable broth (see p. 15)
juice of 1 lime or lemon
12–16 oz. (375–500 g) cellophane, mung bean, rice, or egg noodles
10 garlic cloves, thinly sliced
2 tablespoons vegetable oil
several squares fried tofu, cut into thin strips, or fresh firm tofu, diced
3 hard-boiled eggs, diced
5–8 scallions (spring onions), thinly sliced
2–4 fresh green chili peppers, thinly sliced
1–2 lemons, cut into wedges
small bowl of fresh coriander leaves for sprinkling

In a heavy skillet (frying pan) or wok, sauté the onions, garlic, ginger root, turmeric, curry powder, lemon grass, and cayenne pepper or red chili pepper flakes in the vegetable oil and sesame oil, cooking slowly until the onions are very soft and browned (about 15–20 minutes).

Sprinkle in the chickpea flour, then pour in the coconut milk and the broth. Simmer until the sauce is thickened (about 20 minutes). If it becomes too thick or starts to separate, add a little water. Season with lemon juice and keep warm. Meanwhile, soak and cook the noodles according to the directions on the packet; drain.

To prepare the garnish, sauté the sliced garlic in the vegetable oil until golden brown but not dark and bitter and place on a small plate. Arrange the other garnishes on plates or in bowls. Serve the noodles tossed with the sauce, accompanied by the garnishes.

SERVES 4–6

Cal–Asian Salad

This is fresh and invigorating for a summer lunch.

8 oz. (250 g) thin rice noodles (also called rice sticks or rice vermicelli)
½ Cos lettuce, leaves rolled and cut into thin shreds
½ cucumber, diced
3–5 scallions (spring onions), thinly sliced
pinch of dried mint leaves, crumbled
2 tablespoons olive oil
1 tablespoon lemon juice, or to taste
salt to taste
1 red sweet pepper (capsicum), diced
2 tablespoons slightly crushed peanuts
2 teaspoons sesame oil
5–10 fresh mint leaves
½ teaspoon mild chili pepper powder, or to taste

Soak the rice noodles for 10 minutes, then cook until tender. Drain and rinse in cold water, then set aside.

Combine the lettuce with the cucumber, scallions, and dried mint, then dress with olive oil, lemon juice, and salt. (These steps may be done up to a day ahead and kept, well covered, in the refrigerator.)

Place the green salad in a mound on a serving dish and surround with the noodles. Top with the diced red sweet pepper and crushed peanuts and sprinkle with the sesame oil, fresh mint leaves, and chili pepper powder.

SERVES 3–4

RIGHT ♦ *Cal–Asian Salad*

Baked Pasta

*Baked pasta is usually a hale and hearty affair
emanating comfort and hospitality; great sizzling casseroles filled with vivid flavors and a variety
of ingredients. Their character is completely different from quickly tossed pasta with a simple sauce, or the
light and breezy pasta recipes of summer. Macaroni cheese and lasagne are probably the best-known baked
pasta dishes. Regardless of how many exotic, well-cooked pasta dishes I have eaten, these remain my
favorites, and I frequently make them in endless guises and variations.*

◆ ◆ ◆

*There are fewer fried pasta dishes,
yet occasionally one finds specialities made from fresh noodle dough, fried to a golden crisp and utterly
irresistible. Wontons and egg rolls, stuffed and fried, are such pasta. Unfilled wonton or egg roll noodles, fried
until crispy and golden then sprinkled with icing (confectioners') sugar, make an excellent biscuit- (cookie-)
like sweet, or if sprinkled with savory spices instead of sugar, a cracker-like snack to accompany drinks. Fresh
ravioli, too, can be quickly fried until golden and eaten as an appetizer-like nibble.*

♦ ♦ ♦

Baked Pasta with Mushrooms, Green Beans, Gorgonzola, and Tomatoes

Quite rich, deliciously sloppy, elegant in a very unpretentious way. Nice with a salad of frisée (curly endive) or other young greens and mixed herbs.

12 oz. (375 g) penne, rigatoni, farfalle, seashells, etc.
6 oz. (185 g) green or string beans, cut into
   bite-sized lengths
2 oz. (60 g) butter
2 tablespoons flour
2 cups (16 fl. oz., 500 ml) hot (not boiling) milk
pinch of freshly grated nutmeg
salt and freshly ground black pepper, to taste
8 oz. (250 g) mushrooms, chopped
1 onion, chopped
4 garlic cloves, chopped
8 fresh or tinned tomatoes, diced
1 tablespoon chopped fresh parsley
3 tablespoons tomato paste (purée)
4–5 oz. (125–155 g) Gorgonzola cheese, diced
   or thinly sliced
several tablespoons of freshly grated Parmesan
   cheese, to serve

Cook the pasta until half-done. Add the beans and continue cooking until both are *al dente*, then drain.

Melt half the butter in a pan, then sprinkle in the flour and cook for a few minutes, until the flour is a light golden colour. Remove from the heat, and gradually stir in the milk. Return to the heat and cook, stirring, until the mixture has slightly thickened. Season with nutmeg, salt and pepper and set aside. (This is a béchamel sauce.)

Brown the mushrooms and half the garlic in half the remaining butter. Season with salt and pepper; set aside.

Sauté the tomatoes, the rest of the garlic and the parsley in the remaining butter for about 5 minutes. When tender, add to the béchamel sauce with the tomato paste, the cooked mushrooms, the Gorgonzola cheese, and half the mozzarella cheese.

Mix this with the pasta and beans then pour into a baking dish. Top with the remaining mozzarella cheese and Parmesan cheese, then bake at 375°F (190°C) for 20 minutes, or until the top is melting and lightly browned.

SERVES 4–6

Macaroni and Cheddar Cheese Gratin with Tangy Beet Relish

If you are at my table for a month, you would inevitably be served this crusty-topped macaroni gratin, enlivened with a tangy relish of beet (beetroot) and onions. It is probably my favorite, most comforting dish, perfect for a rainy evening. The relish keeps the dish from being ordinary, and its tanginess lifts the heavier nature of the baked pasta.

1 lb. (500 g) pasta such as farfalle, pennine (small
   quills), elbows, lumachine (seashells), etc.
1 oz. (30 g) butter
2 tablespoons flour
2 cups (16 fl. oz., 500 ml) hot milk
2 garlic cloves, chopped
pinch of freshly grated nutmeg
salt and freshly ground black pepper, to taste
8 oz. (250 g) fresh and blanched, or frozen, peas
14 oz. (435 g) mature Cheddar cheese, grated
1 onion, chopped
4 beets (beetroots), cooked and diced
pinch of sugar or a little honey (optional)
3 teaspoons red or white wine vinegar

Cook the pasta until *al dente*, then drain.

Melt the butter in a saucepan, sprinkle with the flour and cook for a few minutes, then remove from the heat and stir in the milk. Return the saucepan to the heat, and cook, stirring, until the mixture thickens. Season with the garlic, nutmeg, salt and pepper.

Combine the pasta with the sauce, the peas, and three-quarters of the cheese. Spoon into a baking dish and top with the remaining cheese. Bake in the oven at 400°F (200°C) for about 30 minutes, until the cheese topping is crusty and golden.

Meanwhile, prepare the relish: combine the onion, beets, sugar or honey (if using), and vinegar.

Serve each portion of hot baked pasta with a spoonful of the cool tangy relish alongside.

SERVES 4–6

PREVIOUS PAGE ♦ *Baked Pasta with Mushrooms, Green Beans, Gorgonzola, and Tomatoes*

RIGHT ♦ *Macaroni and Cheddar Cheese Gratin with Tangy Beet Relish*

Gratin of Mustard-scented Macaroni and Cheese with Mexican Flavors

This is as distinctive in its seasoning of roasted green sweet pepper (capsicums), Mexican spicing and tangy yogurt as it is deliciously satisfying. A wonderful main course for a winter's evening, preceded by a light and spicy tomato broth and accompanied by a crisp green salad, and maybe some buttery garlic bread.

1 green sweet pepper (caspicum)
12 oz. (375 g) macaroni or other medium
   to large pasta
½ oz. (15 g) butter
1 tablespoon flour
1 cup (8 fl. oz., 250 ml) hot (not boiling) milk
3 tablespoons Greek-style yogurt or sour cream
2 teaspoons mustard of choice or a combination,
   e.g. wholegrain, a mild Dijon
Tabasco or other hot sauce, to taste
½ teaspoon cumin, or to taste
pinch of turmeric

2–3 garlic cloves, chopped
12 oz. (375 g) sharp Cheddar cheese, coarsely grated
salt and freshly ground black pepper and nutmeg,
   to taste
1 teaspoon paprika

Roast the sweet pepper (see p. 19). Slice the peeled flesh into thin strips and set aside.

Cook the pasta until *al dente*, then drain.

Make a béchamel sauce: first heat the butter in a pan, then sprinkle in the flour, and cook for a minute or so. Remove from the heat and stir in the hot milk, then return to the heat and cook, stirring, until the mixture thickens.

Combine the sweet pepper strips, pasta, béchamel sauce, yogurt (or sour cream), mustard, Tabasco or other hot sauce, cumin, turmeric, garlic, cheese, salt, pepper and nutmeg.

Pour into a casserole dish, sprinkle with the paprika, then bake in the oven at 375°F (190°C) for about 40 minutes, until there are golden brown spots on top. Serve immediately.

SERVES 4

Fideos (Mexican-style Thin Pasta with Tomatoes and Cheese)

This recipe for delicious, rather sloppy, messy pasta is very homy, and was taught to me by an exuberant woman from northern Mexico. Thin capellini is cooked in a savory soup-like mixture of tomatoes, broth and vegetables, enlivened with sliced olives and capers, then layered with cheese in a casserole and baked.

2 onions, chopped
1 green sweet pepper (capsicum), sliced
1 red sweet pepper (capsicum), sliced
3 garlic cloves, chopped
2 bay leaves
3 tablespoons vegetable oil
1 teaspoon cumin
1–2 teaspoons mild chili powder, or to taste
½ teaspoon dried oregano
½ teaspoon ground coriander
2 teaspoons paprika
8 oz. (250 g) green or string beans, cut into
   bite-sized lengths
8 oz. (250 g) fresh or frozen peas
1 carrot, diced
14 oz. (435 g) diced fresh or tinned tomatoes
3¾ cups (1½ imp. pints, 900 ml) vegetable broth
   (see p. 15)
12 oz. (375 g) capellini
about 15 pimiento-stuffed green olives, sliced
1 tablespoon capers
several generous shakes of Tabasco sauce
8 oz. (250 g) Cheddar cheese or other sharp
   cheese, coarsely grated or sliced

Sauté the onions, sweet peppers, garlic and bay leaves in the vegetable oil until the onions are softened. Sprinkle with the cumin, chili powder, oregano, coriander and paprika and cook for a few minutes. Add the beans, peas, carrot, tomatoes and broth, and bring to the boil.

Stir in the capellini, then cover the pan and cook over low to medium heat for about 6 minutes, or until the capellini is just tender and the liquid has been absorbed.

Mix in the olives, capers and Tabasco sauce. Layer in a casserole dish with about half the cheese, then top with the remaining cheese.

Bake in the oven at 375°F (190°C) for approximately 30 minutes, or until the cheese is bubbly and golden brown. Serve immediately.

Note: If I have an avocado, I mash it with lemon juice, chopped onion, chopped tomato, chopped chili and fresh coriander leaves to make guacamole, then serve a spoonful or two as a side relish for the baked pasta.

S E R V E S 5

Esther's Apple-Cheese Kugel

Sweet with apple and raisins, and fragrant with cinnamon, this kugel is courtesy of Dr Esther Novak, whose father brought the recipe from Russia. In a lifetime of kugel eating, this is the best I have tasted.
Though sweet, it is traditionally served as part of the main course rather than as a pudding.

12 oz. (375 g) flat noodles, preferably egg noodles,
   or thin vermicelli
3 oz. (90 g) unsalted butter
4 oz. (125 g) cottage cheese
3 large eggs, lightly beaten
2 apples, coarsely grated (do not peel)
2 teaspoons ground cinnamon
8 oz. (250 g) white sugar
6–8 oz. (185–250 g) golden raisins (sultanas)
   or raisins
½ teaspoon baking powder
tiny pinch of salt

Cook the noodles until *al dente,* then drain.

Melt the butter, then combine with the noodles.

Stir in all the remaining ingredients and pour the mixture into a rectangular baking dish.

Bake in the oven at 350°F (180°C) for 1–1½ hours, until brown and crusty. Serve hot or at room temperature.

S E R V E S 4

LEFT ♦ *Gratin of Mustard-scented Macaroni and Cheese with Mexican Flavors*

Lasagne Verde, Venice-style

Anything with peas is a speciality in Venice, so it was no surprise when I found myself in St Mark's Square, face to face with the following delectable lasagne.
Either white or green pasta may be used: I tend to use green lasagne as a contrast to the red tomato sauce and the white béchamel. The colors are those of the Italian flag!

1 oz. (30 g) butter
2 tablespoons flour
2 cups (16 fl. oz., 500 ml) hot (not boiling) milk
salt, freshly ground black pepper and freshly grated nutmeg, to taste
1 onion, chopped
3 garlic cloves, chopped
1 carrot, chopped
2 tablespoons chopped fresh parsley
2 tablespoons olive oil
½ teaspoon each: fennel seeds, dried basil, dried mixed herbs
2 lbs. (1 kg) chopped fresh tomatoes or 2 tins (14 oz., 435 g tins) chopped tomatoes
2 tablespoons tomato paste (purée)
pinch of sugar (optional)
salt and freshly ground black pepper, to taste
1 lb. (500 g) dried or fresh green lasagne
10 oz. (310 g) fresh and blanched or frozen peas
2–3 oz. (60–90 g) Parmesan cheese, freshly grated
12 oz. (375 g) mozzarella or other mild white cheese, thinly sliced or grated
1 tablespoon olive oil
½ teaspoon dried thyme

To make the béchamel sauce, melt the butter in a heavy saucepan over a medium heat, then sprinkle in the flour. Cook for a few minutes, until the flour is lightly colored, then remove from the heat and gradually stir in the milk. Return to the heat and cook, stirring, over a medium heat, until the mixture has thickened. Season with salt, pepper and nutmeg. Set aside.

To make the tomato sauce, sauté the onion, garlic, carrot, and parsley in the olive oil for a few minutes, until the onion is softened, then add the fennel seeds, basil, dried mixed herbs, tomatoes, tomato paste, sugar (if using) and salt and pepper. Simmer for 10 minutes, or until well flavored. Set aside.

If using dried pasta, cook it in plenty of boiling, salted water until *al dente*, then drain carefully, so as not to break up the sheets. If using fresh pasta, do not cook, but pour a little water over the top of the prepared dish and bake 20 minutes longer.

To assemble, ladle several spoonfuls (a third) of the tomato sauce into the bottom of a baking dish then top with a quarter of the lasagne sheets, letting the sheets rise up the side of the dish. Then ladle in half the béchamel sauce, half the peas, and a generous amount of the Parmesan. Next add another quarter of the pasta, another layer of tomato sauce (the next third) and half the mozzarella. Top with another quarter of pasta, the remaining béchamel and peas, then the final layer of pasta. Top with the last of the tomato sauce, and the remaining mozzarella and Parmesan. Drizzle the olive oil over and add a sprinkling of thyme.

Bake in the oven at 400°F (200°C) (lower the heat if it shows signs of burning) for 45 minutes, or until the top is browned and melting.

VARIATION

Jenny's Eggplant and Red Sweet Pepper Lasagne Verde: Our young family friend, Jenny Wight, is as keen a cook and pasta-eater as we are. Recently she served us a delicious lasagne filled with eggplant (aubergine) and red sweet peppers (capsicums). To prepare, follow the recipe above, but substitute one layer of sliced sautéed eggplant and one layer of sautéed or roasted and peeled sweet peppers for the peas.

SERVES 6–8

Spinach and Ricotta Lasagne

The filling for this lasagne also makes excellent cannelloni, easily thrown together with egg-roll wrappers, which do not need to be precooked, and are tender and delicate.

2 onions, chopped
3 garlic cloves, chopped
2 tablespoons chopped fresh parsley
3 tablespoons olive oil
½ teaspoon fennel seeds
½ teaspoon dried thyme or mixed herbs
4 cups (1¾ imp. pints, 1 litre) tomato purée (passata)
3–4 tablespoons tomato paste (purée)
½ teaspoon sugar (optional)
salt and freshly ground black pepper, to taste
12 oz. (375 g) cooked spinach, squeezed dry
1½ lbs. (750 g) ricotta cheese
1 egg, lightly beaten
4 oz. (125 g) Parmesan cheese, freshly grated
8 oz. (250 g) lasagne
6–8 oz. (185–250 g) mozzarella cheese, thinly
    sliced or grated

Sauté the onions, half the garlic and the parsley in 2 tablespoons of the olive oil until they are softened. Add the fennel seeds, dried herbs, tomato purée and tomato paste and bring to the boil. Reduce the heat and simmer for about 5 minutes, or until the sauce has thickened. Season with sugar, and salt and pepper, then set aside.

Sauté the remaining garlic in the remaining oil, then add the cooked spinach and cook for a minute or two. Mix in the ricotta, egg, and about three-quarters of the Parmesan, and season with salt and pepper. Set aside.

Cook the lasagne in plenty of boiling, salted water until *al dente*, then drain carefully, so that the pasta sheets do not stick together or break.

Layer about a third of the pasta in a shallow baking dish, then top with about half the tomato sauce, then another layer of pasta, then the spinach and cheese mixture. Place the final layer of pasta on top of this, then spoon on the remaining tomato sauce. Top with the mozzarella cheese, sprinkle with the remaining Parmesan, then bake in the oven at 375°F (190°C) for about 45 minutes, or until the top is browned.

SERVES 4–6

Rachel's Homely and Comforting Macaroni and Spinach Dish

This casserole was prepared for me by my friend Rachel Wight at a time when she knew I needed something comforting and cosy. It is not innovative or glamorous, but it is enormously comforting, the sort of dish that makes you feel extremely well cared for.
You can vary the cheese used as desired; I've eaten similar dishes in Italy made with fontina cheese, and in North America where the cheese was Monterey Jack. The important thing is that the spinach is fresh, and that you are in the proper mood. If you feel like making a richer dish, top the casserole with buttered breadcrumbs before baking. And if you feel like something spicy, add hot pepper sauce or Tabasco.

12 oz. (375 g) elbow or other small macaroni
1–2 bunches fresh spinach
1½ oz. (45 g) butter
1 tablespoon flour
1 cup (8 fl. oz., 250 ml) hot (not boiling) milk
salt, cayenne pepper and freshly grated nutmeg,
    to taste
8 oz. (250 g) Cheddar or other sharp cheese,
    shredded
3 oz. (90 g) Parmesan cheese, freshly grated
2 hard-boiled eggs, diced
a little paprika to serve (optional)

Cook the pasta until *al dente*; drain. Cook the spinach until just tender, then drain and squeeze dry.

Make a béchamel sauce: melt a third of the butter in a pan then sprinkle in the flour. Cook for a few minutes, until the flour is lightly golden, then remove from the heat and gradually stir in the milk. Return to the heat and cook, stirring, until the mixture thickens. Season with salt, cayenne pepper, and nutmeg. Set aside.

Dot the bottom of a baking dish with a little of the remaining butter, then cover with half the macaroni. Top with the spinach, half the béchamel sauce, half the cheeses and half the hard-boiled eggs, then top with the remaining macaroni, butter, hard-boiled egg, béchamel sauce and cheeses. Bake in the oven at 400°F (200°C), until the top is golden brown. Serve immediately, sprinkled with a little paprika (if using).

SERVES 4

Baked Penne or Farfalle with Asparagus and Fontina

When asparagus is out of season, replace with sugar snap peas or slices of blanched artichoke heart.

1 lb. (500 g) penne or farfalle
1 lb. (500 g) asparagus, tough ends broken off and discarded, the spears cut into bite-sized lengths
2 oz. (60 g) butter
2 tablespoons flour
1 cup (8 fl. oz., 250 ml) hot (not boiling) milk
1 cup (8 fl. oz., 250 ml) hot vegetable broth (see p. 15)
salt and freshly ground black pepper and nutmeg, to taste
12 oz. (375 g) fontina cheese, grated
4 oz. (125 g) Parmesan cheese, freshly grated
2 garlic cloves, chopped (optional)

Cook the pasta until half done, then add the asparagus and continue cooking until both are *al dente*. Drain, toss with a quarter of the butter, and set aside.

Heat 2 tablespoons of the butter in a pan, then sprinkle in the flour and cook for a few minutes, until the flour is lightly golden. Remove from the heat, gradually stir in the milk, then the broth. Return to a medium heat and cook, stirring, for about 2 minutes, until thickened. Season with salt, pepper, and nutmeg.

Combine the pasta and asparagus with the sauce, then add two-thirds of the fontina cheese and several spoonfuls of the Parmesan cheese and garlic (if using). Pour into a baking dish and cover with the remaining fontina cheese, then sprinkle with the remaining Parmesan cheese and dot with the remaining butter.

Bake in the oven at 375°F (190°C) for 30 minutes, or until the cheese topping is melted and golden.

SERVES 4–6

Casserole of Eggplant and Small Pasta with Ricotta and Mozzarella Cheese

Serve this hearty casserole with a light and tangy salad of arugula (rocket) and a milder young lettuce.

2 eggplants (aubergines), sliced
olive oil, for frying
1 lb. (500 g) small seashell pasta or other small pasta such as anellini (little rings)
4 garlic cloves, chopped
¼–½ teaspoon fennel seeds
large pinch of dried oregano
3¾ cups (1½ imp. pints, 900 ml) tomato purée (passata)
pinch of sugar
salt and freshly ground black pepper, to taste
8–12 oz. (250–375 g) ricotta cheese
8 oz. (250 g) mozzarella cheese, thinly sliced
4 oz. (125 g) Parmesan cheese, freshly grated, plus extra, to serve

Fry or sauté the eggplant slices in a single layer in a small amount of oil until they are browned and tender. Cook in batches if necessary. Set aside.

Cook the pasta until *al dente*, then drain. Rinse with cold water and set aside.

Sauté the garlic and fennel seeds in about 2 tablespoons of olive oil, then add the oregano and tomato purée and season with sugar, salt and pepper. Simmer for about 10 minutes.

Layer half the eggplant in a baking dish.

Mix the pasta with three-quarters of the tomato sauce, then spoon into the baking dish. Top with the remaining eggplant. Dot with the ricotta, then cover with the mozzarella cheese, remaining tomato sauce and a sprinkling of Parmesan.

Bake in the oven at 375°F (190°C) for approximately 35 minutes, until the cheese is bubbling and lightly browned.

SERVES 6

RIGHT ♦ *Baked Penne or Farfalle with Asparagus and Fontina*

Stuffed Pasta and Dumplings

These days, all kinds of shops abound with fresh or dried stuffed pasta.
The pasta used is often plain egg dough, but might also be green from spinach or herbs, pink from tomato or red sweet pepper (capsicum), dusty brown from mushrooms, or yellow from saffron. The fillings range from simple ricotta to spinach, asparagus, artichoke, mushrooms, even spiced mashed potato.
Stuffed pasta only needs a simple sauce, to complement its filling: float a handful of stuffed pasta in a simple broth or toss it with melted butter and lots of fragrant chopped herbs or grated cheese.

◆ ◆ ◆

Stuffed pasta makes a good main course, too.
Mix and match vegetable-stuffed pasta with vegetable sauces: mushroom-filled tortellini in asparagus cream, or asparagus-stuffed ravioli in mushroom cream. Or combine different types of stuffed pasta into one dish to make the meal a sort of treasure hunt (buy the pasta loose). Try creating your own stuffed pastas, too, from home-made pasta dough (see p. 12), or using wonton wrappers. There is a whole range of unusual dumpling-like pastas too, seldom available in supermarkets, and they taste wonderful.

Mushroom Ravioli with Summer Squash, Mushrooms, and Sun-dried Tomato-Garlic Broth

6 garlic cloves, 5 coarsely cut up and 1 finely chopped
1 cup (8 fl. oz., 250 ml) vegetable broth (see p. 15)
2 summer squash, preferably yellow zucchini (courgettes) or crookneck, or ordinary green zucchini, diced
about 8 sun-dried tomatoes, cut into strips
6 oz. (185 g) mushrooms, thinly sliced
½ oz. (15 g) butter or 1 tablespoon oil
12–16 oz. (375–500 g) mushroom-stuffed pasta
8 oz. (250 g) mild white cheese such as a mild Cheddar, mozzarella or fontina, diced
1 tablespoon finely chopped fresh parsley

Combine the coarsely cut up garlic with the broth and bring to the boil. Cook over a high heat until the garlic is tender and the liquid is reduced by at least half. Add the squash or zucchini and sun-dried tomatoes and continue cooking until the squash is tender and the liquid even further reduced and intensified in flavor.

Quickly brown the mushrooms in the butter or oil and set aside.

Cook the pasta until *al dente*, then drain. Combine with the reserved vegetable mixture, sautéed mushrooms, cheese, and finely chopped garlic. Toss together until the cheese melts, heating it over a medium flame if necessary.

Serve immediately, sprinkled with the parsley.

S E R V E S   4 – 6

PREVIOUS PAGE ♦ *Mushroom Ravioli with Summer Squash, Mushrooms, and Sun-dried Tomato–Garlic Broth (left), and Tortelloni in Broth with Green Vegetables and Herbs (right)*
RIGHT ♦ *Cheese Ravioli with Crisp-fried Sage Leaves and Tomato Coulis*

Tortelloni in Broth with Green Vegetables and Herbs

12 oz. (375 g) fresh tortelloni, such as green pasta filled with ricotta cheese
4 cups (1¾ imp. pints, 1 litre) vegetable broth (see p. 15)
1 bunch broccoli, cut into florets, or 2 zucchini (courgettes), diced, or a handful of peas, or a handful of green or string beans, chopped, or any combination of green vegetables
2 tablespoons olive oil
2 tablespoons chopped fresh chives
1 tablespoon chopped fresh mixed herbs such as marjoram, sage, oregano, etc.

Cook the tortelloni until *al dente*; drain and set aside.

Combine the broth with the vegetables in a pan and bring to the boil. Cook until the vegetables are bright green and just tender.

Mix the olive oil, chives and mixed herbs together.

Add the tortelloni to the broth and serve immediately, garnishing each portion with a spoonful of the herby oil.

S E R V E S   6

Cheese Ravioli with Crisp-fried Sage Leaves and Tomato Coulis

25–30 fresh sage leaves (they must be fresh)
5 tablespoons olive oil
1 lb. (500 g) fresh cheese-stuffed ravioli
salt and freshly ground black pepper, to taste
4–6 ripe tomatoes, diced
2–3 tablespoons freshly grated Parmesan cheese, to serve

Fry the sage leaves in the olive oil until they are just crisp. Remove from the heat and set aside.

Cook the ravioli until *al dente*, then drain.

Drizzle the oil and sage leaves over the hot ravioli, season with salt and pepper, then sprinkle with the diced tomatoes. Serve immediately with the Parmesan cheese.

S E R V E S   4 – 6

Mushroom Ravioli with Beet and Tomato Purée

*This sauce is Fauvist pink, the color of hot neon —
fascinating and slightly intimidating. The taste is lovely, with
the delicate sweetness of beets (beetroot) paired with slightly
acidic tomatoes, all smoothed out with a little cream. Splash
it onto mushroom ravioli or toss it with little elbow shapes.*

1 large beet (beetroot), cooked but not pickled
8 ripe tomatoes, peeled and diced, or 8 oz.
   (250 g) tinned tomatoes
1 small onion, chopped
5 fl. oz. (155 ml) light (single) cream
squeeze of lemon juice
salt and freshly ground black pepper, to taste
12 oz. (375 g) mushroom-stuffed ravioli
1 oz. (30 g) butter
4 oz. (125 g) dolcelatte cheese, crumbled, or a
   combination of crumbled Gorgonzola and
   mascarpone
8–10 fresh basil leaves, thinly sliced

Dice the beet and combine this with the tomatoes and
onion in a blender (liquidizer) or food processor. Blend
until smooth, then add the cream and continue to blend
until well mixed.

Season well with lemon juice, salt and pepper and
pour into a saucepan or skillet (frying pan).

Heat the sauce for just a few minutes, or until it
darkens slightly in color. Remove from the heat.

Meanwhile cook the pasta until *al dente*, then drain.
Toss the pasta with the butter, then with the hot sauce.
Serve immediately, sprinkled with the cheese and basil.

VARIATION

For a slightly different flavor, don't cook the sauce, but
toss it directly with the hot buttered pasta. It will be
slightly sweeter, with the uncooked onion showing
through in a more pronounced way.

SERVES 4

Fresh Herb and Edible Flower Pasta

Sandwich a layer of herbs and/or flower petals between two pieces of pasta dough or wonton wrappers and you have a delicate pasta that is not only beautiful, but delicious too. The pasta shapes — triangles, rectangles, diamonds or circles — look opaque and starchy when raw, but when cooked they are transformed into little gems, almost like stained glass. Any herb leaves and unsprayed edible flowers will do: fennel sprigs, coriander, thyme, oregano or marjoram leaves, flat-leaf (Italian) parsley, even a selection of herbs are all beautiful once trapped between the sheets of translucent pasta. The addition of edible flower petals adds a colorful note; try sage leaves combined with purple sage blossom petals or chives and their lavender-hued blossoms. Nasturtiums are particularly fetching with their vivid colors, but their strong flavor makes them more than a colorful accent; prepare them with an assortment of other herbs rather than on their own. Follow the basic recipe below and invent your own herb or flower fillings. Admittedly they take a bit of time to assemble, but these stunning pastas are easily made, and are particularly convenient if you use wonton or egg-roll wrappers, available from Asian food stores.

fresh herbs such as flat-leaf (Italian) parsley,
    coriander, sage, marjoram, oregano, thyme,
    fennel or dill sprigs, tarragon leaves, rosemary
    needles, etc. and/or edible blossom petals
2 teaspoons cornstarch (cornflour)
2 tablespoons water
about 12 oz. (375 g) wonton or egg roll wrappers

Cut the leaves from the stems and remove the petals from any blossoms. Rinse and dry both.

Mix the cornstarch with the water. Take 1 piece of dough and brush it with this mixture, then quickly arrange a single layer of a few herbs and/or flower petals on it, taking care to leave at least a ¼ in (6 mm) border. Cover quickly with another equal-sized piece of pasta and press together well to eliminate any trapped air. For best results roll the filled dough with a rolling pin.

Place on a board that you have dusted well with cornstarch or flour and repeat. When you have prepared a complete layer of filled pasta, cover with a piece of cling film (plastic wrap) before adding another layer.

These ravioli are delicate and beautiful rather than hearty and filling: allow 5 filled ravioli per person as a first course.

Cook carefully in gently boiling salted water, doing them in several batches to keep them from sticking together. They cook in about 2 to 3 minutes. Lift them out with a slotted spoon. Place on a hot platter and toss with melted butter or follow one of the serving suggestions below.

Ravioli Stuffed with Ricotta, Herbs, and Black Olives

Ricotta cheese is creamy but not rich. Here its blandness is balanced by pungent and salty black olives and fragrant herbs.

1 lb. (500 g) ricotta cheese
1 oz. (30 g) Parmesan cheese, freshly grated
3 garlic cloves, finely chopped
2 teaspoons fresh chopped thyme or rosemary
about 25 black olives (kalamata, oil-cured), pitted
    and diced
2 eggs, lightly beaten
1 packet wonton wrappers, or 1 quantity fresh pasta
    dough (see p. 12), rolled and cut into squares
1 oz. (30 g) butter
several thinly sliced fresh basil leaves, or large
    pinches of fresh thyme leaves

Mix the ricotta with the Parmesan, garlic, thyme (or rosemary), olives, and eggs.

Place a tablespoon or so of this filling into the center of each wonton wrapper or pasta square, then brush the edges with water. Top with another wonton wrapper or pasta square, then press well to seal. Leave on a lightly floured plate or baking sheet for about 30 minutes.

Boil the wontons gently until *al dente*, about 3–4 minutes. Place several pasta in the saucepan to start, then wait a moment, then add several more; this will help keep the pasta from cooking into one large lump. Drain carefully, removing the pasta from the pan using a slotted spoon so the pasta does not break apart.

Serve immediately, tossed in the butter and basil (or thyme).

SERVES ABOUT 6

LEFT ♦ *Fresh Herb and Edible Flower Pasta*

Potato Gnocchi

While you can purchase locally made and imported potato gnocchi, they are easy and inexpensive to make yourself. The finest potato gnocchi I have ever tasted were made with yellow Finnish potatoes, whose flesh was dry and mealy. I find that the water content in our potatoes makes preparing predictable gnocchi virtually impossible. If the potatoes are too moist, it will be leaden and gummy; too dry and you might have heavy dumplings. The problem is caused by the water needed to boil the potatoes before they are mashed. You can eliminate this by baking your potatoes. The second method for excellent gnocchi is a surprising one: dehydrated instant mashed potatoes. It is surprising how well the dumplings turn out. Serve these luscious little dumplings with a light garlicky tomato sauce such as the one for Tricolor Conchiglie with Garlic and Tomato Sauce (p. 78) or with Lusty Tomato and Pea Sauce (p. 119). If you do want to use fresh potatoes, use 2 lbs. (1 kg) yellow Finnish or 1 lb. (500 g) each of baking potatoes and waxy red or white ones.

2 lbs. (1 kg) baking potatoes or 1 packet
   (3 oz., 90 g) dehydrated mashed potatoes
1 egg, lightly beaten
about 16 oz. (500 g) all-purpose (plain) unbleached
   flour
a little butter
sauce of choice (see above)
freshly grated Parmesan cheese, to serve

Bake the potatoes until tender. Cool them so that you are able to handle them, then remove and mash their soft flesh. If using dehydrated potatoes, rehydrate with boiling water according to the directions on the packet. Stir well and leave to cool to room temperature.

Add the egg and half the flour and mix well, kneading as you would bread. But take care, because too much kneading will make the gnocchi tough. The batter should be soft, yet hold its shape. Add the remaining flour as needed to achieve the correct consistency.

Break the dough into chunks about the size of an apricot. With floured hands, gently roll each chunk out into a cylinder about ¾ in (2 cm) thick, then, using a sharp knife, cut off short, squat lengths. Carefully lay the finished dumplings out on a floured board as you cut them. Leave to dry for at least 15 minutes.

Bring a large pan of water to the boil, then add the gnocchi, in several batches. Immediately turn the heat down to a simmer (too violent a boil will break the tender dumplings apart). When they are ready, after about 4–6 minutes, they will float to the surface.

Remove with a slotted spoon, drain thoroughly, then place on a baking sheet or serving platter. Either serve immediately, tossed in butter and splashed with a sauce, or leave for 30–60 minutes to settle and firm up. I like the gnocchi best when they have had a chance to settle.

When ready to serve, heat the sauce and layer with the gnocchi in a baking dish. Top with grated Parmesan cheese and heat in a hot oven until the cheese melts. Serve immediately.

SERVES 4–6

Ravioli with Sugar Snap Peas, Summer Squash, Chard, and Basil

3–4 oz. (90–125 g) sugar snap peas
2 summer squash, preferably golden zucchini
   (courgettes) or yellow crookneck, or ordinary
   green zucchini, cut into bite-sized pieces
10–15 leaves chard (silver beet), cut into thin
   ribbons
5–8 sun-dried tomatoes, cut into strips (optional)
3–5 garlic cloves, chopped
4–5 tablespoons olive oil or 2 oz. (60 g) butter
handful of fresh basil leaves, thinly sliced
12 oz. (375 g) fresh ravioli, preferably stuffed with
   ricotta cheese
2 oz. (60 g) Parmesan cheese, freshly grated,
   or to taste
salt and freshly ground black pepper, to taste

Blanch the vegetables, including the tomatoes (if using), until crisp-tender; this may be done in one pan and should take about 4 minutes. Drain and set aside, reserving the water for cooking the pasta.

Sauté the garlic in the olive oil or butter until it is golden. Add the blanched vegetables and toss briefly, then add the basil and set aside. Keep warm.

Meanwhile boil the pasta (in the reserved water) until *al dente*. Drain and toss with the vegetables. Add the Parmesan, salt and pepper. Serve immediately.

SERVES 4–6

Potato Ravioli with Tomatoes and Thyme

It might sound unlikely, but potato-filled ravioli are sublime. The bright nuggets of diced fresh tomatoes and lashing of thyme-flavored butter give it spark.

1 lb. (500 g) baking potatoes, peeled and diced
2 oz. (60 g) Parmesan cheese, freshly grated
1 egg, lightly beaten
a little milk (optional)
salt and freshly ground black pepper, to taste
5 scallions (spring onions), thinly sliced
1 packet wonton wrappers, or 1 quantity fresh pasta
   dough (see p. 12), cut into squares or circles
3 oz. (90 g) butter
2 teaspoons fresh thyme, or ½ teaspoon crumbled
   dried thyme
1 lb. (500 g) ripe tomatoes, peeled, seeded and
   diced

Boil the potatoes until tender; drain and mash. Mix in Parmesan cheese, egg, and milk to thin as needed. Season with salt and pepper and add scallions. Set aside to cool.

Place 1 heaped tablespoon of the potato mixture in the centre of each wonton wrapper or pasta piece. Brush the edges with water, and top with another piece. Dust lightly with flour and set aside on a floured board for 30 minutes. (These can be made and frozen for up to two months. Place in single layer on baking sheets lined with waxed paper, and freeze. Do not thaw before cooking.)

Cook the wontons (in several batches) in a large pan of boiling water until just tender (about 2 minutes if fresh and 5 minutes if frozen). Transfer to plates using a slotted spoon. Keep warm by lightly covering with foil.

Meanwhile, melt the butter in a small heavy skillet (frying pan) over a medium heat. Mix in the thyme and spoon over the ravioli. Garnish with the diced tomatoes.

Serves 4

ABOVE ♦ *Potato Gnocchi*

Crisp-fried Tofu and Shiitake Wonton with Ginger Sweet–Sour Sauce

Tofu, shiitake mushrooms and cloud ear fungus make a light wonton filling, served with a classic sweet–sour sauce. You could also make a sauce with soy sauce, vinegar and hot chili oil, thinned out with a little of the mushroom soaking liquid and seasoned with finely chopped fresh coriander leaves.

6–8 dried shiitake (Chinese black mushrooms)
2 large cloud ear or tree cloud fungus
8 oz. (250 g) tofu, either regular or firm
3 scallions (spring onions), thinly sliced
2 tablespoons chopped fresh coriander leaves
8–10 fresh and blanched or tinned water chestnuts, chopped
1 tablespoon soy sauce
1 tablespoon sesame oil
1 packet wonton wrappers or similar fresh noodles
1 egg, beaten
oil, for deep frying

Ginger Sweet–Sour Sauce:
2 oz. (60 g) dark brown demerara sugar
1 tablespoon cornstarch (cornflour)
¾ cup (6 fl. oz., 185 ml) pineapple juice
2 tablespoons tomato ketchup
1 tablespoon chopped fresh ginger root
½ teaspoon salt, or to taste
2–3 fl. oz. (60–90 ml) white wine vinegar, or to taste

Rehydrate the shiitake and cloud ear fungus in hot water (see p. 17). Remove the stems and tough bits from the mushrooms and fungus, then chop finely.

Mash the tofu and mix it with the mushrooms, fungus, scallions, water chestnuts, soy sauce, and sesame oil.

Place about a teaspoon of the filling in the center of each wonton. Brush a little beaten egg round the edges of each noodle and bring two diagonally-opposed corners together, and press to seal. You will now have a triangle shape. Wet each of the other two corners with a dab of water, then seal them together, to form the traditional wonton shape. Set aside for at least 10 minutes.

Deep-fry until golden (about 2 minutes); remove and drain on absorbent paper. Serve immediately, with Ginger Sweet–Sour Sauce).

Put the sugar, cornstarch, pineapple juice, ketchup, ginger root and salt into a pan. Cook over a medium heat until the mixture thickens.

Season to taste with the vinegar, adjusting the sweet–sour balance if necessary.

Serve at room temperature with the fried wontons.

MAKES ABOUT 50 WONTONS, TO SERVE 6–8

Spätzle

These tiny dumplings are hearty, yet delicate, and very versatile — warm them in garlic butter, season them with saffron, toss them with spring or autumn vegetables — and they are so easy to prepare it is ridiculous.

8–10 oz. (250–310 g) all-purpose (plain) flour
1 teaspoon salt
2 large eggs
½ cup (4 fl. oz., 125 ml) milk
a little butter or olive oil
chopped garlic or fresh herbs, to serve

Combine the flour and salt in a bowl and set aside.

In another bowl, beat the eggs with the milk. Combine this with the flour to make a sticky, doughy batter.

Bring a large pan of salted water to the boil, then seat a colander — the type with very large holes — over the boiling pot, pour in the dough and, using a large spoon, force it through the holes. The dough will form squiggly dumpling shapes eventually; when you are forcing it through, however, it will fall like straggling lumps and seem more like a mess than a prospective dinner.

Cover the pan, ignoring the fact that it looks very messy, and boil over medium to high heat for 5 minutes. Release the lid if it threatens to boil over.

Drain carefully and place the dumplings in a bowl of cold water to firm up. Leave for 15–20 minutes; do not be tempted to omit this step or they will be gummy.

To serve, reheat the spätzle in a small amount of hot butter or olive oil, seasoned with a little chopped garlic and/or herbs.

SERVES 4

RIGHT ◆ *Crisp-fried Tofu and Shiitake Wonton with Ginger Sweet–Sour Sauce*

Spätzle with Browned Onions, Dried Mushrooms, and Rosemary

½–1 oz. (15–30 g) dried mushrooms, such as
    porcini, shiitake, etc.
12 fl. oz. (375 ml) hot, but not boiling, water or
    vegetable broth (see p. 15)
2 onions, chopped
3 garlic cloves, coarsely chopped (optional)
butter or oil, for sautéeing
1 x recipe for Spätzle (see p. 170), cooked, soaked
    and drained
salt and freshly ground black pepper, to taste
2 tablespoons chopped fresh rosemary leaves

Rehydrate the dried mushrooms in the hot water or broth (see p. 15), reserving the liquid. Cut into fairly small pieces.

Sauté the onions and garlic (if using) in butter or oil until they are golden, then add the mushrooms. Heat through, then add the spätzle. Add extra butter or oil if needed to keep the dumplings from falling apart. Season with salt and pepper.

Pour ⅓–⅔ cup (3–5 fl. oz., 90–155 ml) of the mushroom-soaking liquid into the pan and cook over medium to high heat until it has reduced.

Serve immediately, each portion sprinkled with fresh rosemary.

SERVES 4

Ravioli Stuffed with Broccoli and Goat Cheese

While these plump little parcels could be simply tossed with butter or cream, or a little tomato sauce, I like garlic butter and fresh rosemary.

5 garlic cloves, 2 coarsely chopped, 3 finely chopped
1 tablespoon olive oil
small pinch of hot red pepper flakes
6 oz. (185 g) broccoli, cooked and coarsely chopped
8–12 oz. (250–375 g) goat cheese, crumbled
1 oz. (30 g) Parmesan cheese, freshly grated
pinch of nutmeg
2 eggs, lightly beaten
salt, to taste
1 packet wonton wrappers, or 1 quantity fresh pasta
    dough (see p. 12, rolled and cut into squares
1 oz. (30 g) butter
3 tablespoons chopped fresh rosemary

Lightly sauté the coarsely chopped garlic in the olive oil with the hot red pepper flakes, until the garlic turns golden.

Toss the cooked broccoli with the garlic and oil, then mix in the goat cheese, Parmesan, nutmeg, eggs and salt.

Place a tablespoon or so of this mixture in the centre of each wonton wrapper or pasta square. Brush the edges with water, top with another piece of pasta, seal the edges well, then leave on a floured board to dry and to stick the edges together, for about 30 minutes. If chilling for later use, reflour the plate and check occasionally that the moisture from the filling has not soaked through. Flour again as needed.

Boil the wontons gently until *al dente*, about 3–4 minutes (you may want to add the pasta several at a time, wait a moment than add several more; this will help keep the pasta from cooking into one large lump). Drain carefully, removing the pasta from the pan using a slotted spoon so the pasta does not break apart.

Melt the butter in a pan, then remove from the heat and add the finely chopped garlic. Pour over the ravioli and serve immediately, sprinkled with the rosemary.

SERVES 4–6

Index

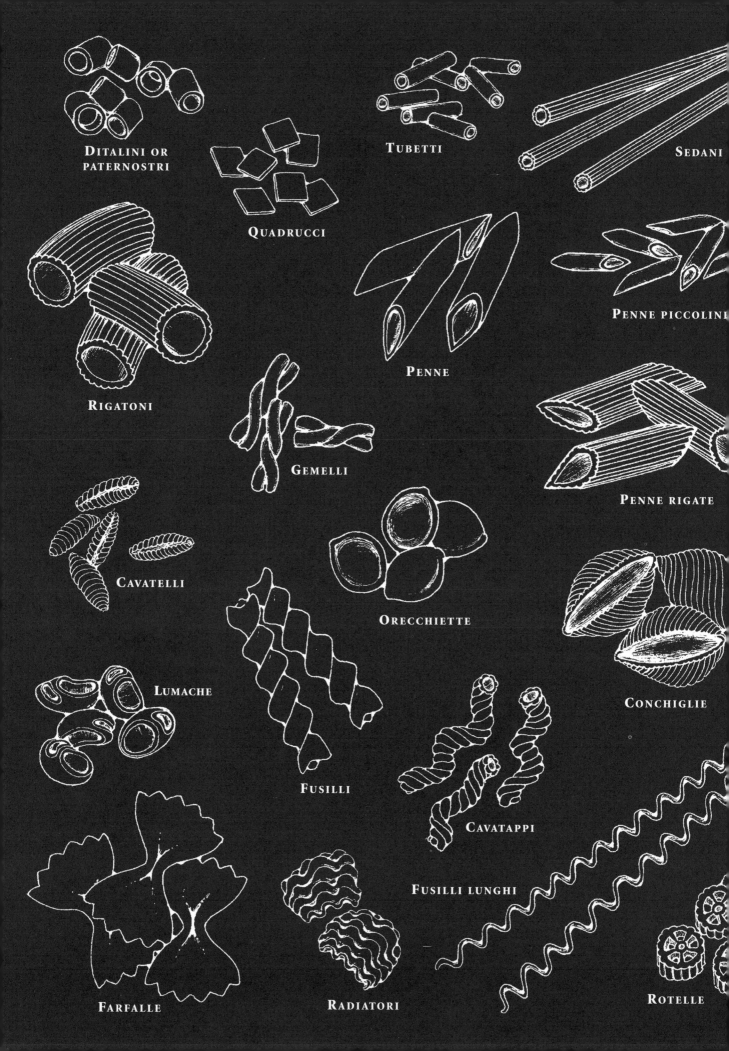

DITALINI OR PATERNOSTRI

QUADRUCCI

TUBETTI

SEDANI

RIGATONI

PENNE PICCOLINI

PENNE

GEMELLI

PENNE RIGATE

CAVATELLI

ORECCHIETTE

CONCHIGLIE

LUMACHE

FUSILLI

CAVATAPPI

FARFALLE

RADIATORI

FUSILLI LUNGHI

ROTELLE